Finding Me In The Mess

FINDING ME IN THE MESS

EMILY STRICKLAND

This book is based on true events, but any reference to events, real people, or real places have been changed and altered to protect their identity. Also, please note that I am not a doctor of any sort and this book in no way can take away from the help an actual doctor can provide you. This is simply a part of a testimony of my own life and a view from my standpoint on my teenage and young adult life and what helped me to change personally.

Copyright ©2016 by Emily K. Strickland. All rights reserved.

This book or any portion thereof may not be reproduced or used in any manner whatsoever without the express written permission of the publisher except for the use of brief quotations in a book review.

Printed in the United States of America

First Printing, 2016

ISBN 978-1523485795

Createspace Publishing

Any and all references or actual Bible verses are from the King James Version, unless otherwise notated within the book.

Scriptures in bold and italicized by author only for added emphasis.

Scripture taken from the New King James version®. Copyright © 1982 by Thomas Nelson. Used by permission. All rights reserved.

Holy Bible, New Living Translation, copyright © 1996, 2004, 2015 by Tyndale House Foundation. Used by permission of Tyndale House Publishers INC., Carol Stream, Illinois 60188. All rights reserved.

Holy Bible, New International Version®, NIV® Copyright ©1973, 1978, 1984, 2011 by Biblica, Inc.® Used by permission. All rights reserved worldwide.

The Holy Bible, New Century Version®. Copyright © 2005 by Thomas Nelson, Inc.

All definitions come from the Webster dictionary online.

Dedication

This book is dedicated to my father, Frank Moss; I never would have fallen so deeply in love with the English language and writing without you. You instilled in me a love for everything written from a young age. Thank you for helping nurture this gift inside of me. I know that you are no longer alive to witness what I have accomplished, but I want you to know that I am thankful for what you helped grow inside of me; I am able to write because of your tutelage. You are an inspiration Daddy!! I know you are smiling right now, and I know that everything that I am is highly do to who you were here on earth. This one is for you Dad!!!!

As well, I am dedicating this to my husband Chazdon, thank you for your love for me. You took the time to help me clean up the mess and find me. I love you always and forever!!!

Contents

Foreword by Pastor Tammy Brunk……………………1

Introduction……………………………………………4

Chapter 1………………………………………………9

Chapter 2………………………………………………21

Chapter 3………………………………………………35

Chapter 4………………………………………………49

Chapter 5………………………………………………63

Chapter 6………………………………………………77

Chapter 7………………………………………………91

Chapter 8………………………………………………105

Chapter 9………………………………………………119

Chapter 10……………………………………………133

Epilogue………………………………………………149

Poetry…………………………………………………152

A Call To Repentance…………………………………162

Acknowledgements……………………………………163

About the Author………………………………………165

they see me, then that's who I must be." Through the revealing of root issues in our lives we can begin our process of freedom, our process of coming into who we were created to be through Christ Jesus. As we find ourselves in a heap of ashes, our Father is so faithful to restore us and give us our beauty back. He gives us confidence through Him and our image reflects who He created us to be, making us pure and whole once again.

My prayer as you read this book, is that you hear the heart of the Father for your life. This book blessed me and brought further healing. We are all on this journey and it's a blessing when we can bring healing through our lives to each other in the body of Christ. "Women healing women."

Tammy Brunk

Awakening Harvest Inc./Tammy Brunk ministries

Author of "Born Identity"

Foreword

Emily Strickland is a beautiful woman of God, wife, mother of four and wonderful friend. She takes a bold stand in areas every young girl and woman faces throughout their lives. As she shares her story, she takes the reader on a transparent journey in order to bring freedom to those in bondage and healing to those that are broken.

So many of us can relate in one way or another to Emily's story. As women, we have faced low-self-esteem, lack of confidence, rejection, shame and guilt. Maybe right now this is your story! You're living this in different ways, day-after-day, and you're ready for a change! You're ready to become the person you were purposed to be. Jesus came for those whose lives were in turmoil. Where one choice had led them into so many choices they never intended to make. He came for our brokenness and rejection, where we have been used and abused. Through all our mess! He rescues us! He heals our wounds and takes our broken shattered lives and puts us back together again to make us whole.

In so many ways the world has objectified women and it's uncanny. The heart, emotions and inner turmoil of what so many young girls growing up have experienced are magnified, broken down and defined throughout each chapter of this book. Jesus did not come to objectify women. When He came as God, as man, He brought healing and revealed the value of a woman. He stood up for women in a culture that degraded women and made them second class citizens. He is standing up for you! Where there is injustice, He wants to bring justice. Where there is rejection, He wants you to know you are accepted, loved, and valued. You are not an object! You are a living, created daughter of God our Father. He holds your book, where He has written about your life! He wants to reveal to you the purpose and plan He has for you on this earth.

As we are brought into root issues, we realize that shame and guilt will always work against our God given Identity and try to reshape and define us differently. They will work against our created image and make us a reflection of how the world defines us. "If that's how

INTRODUCTION

"Cast *not away therefore your confidence, which hath great recompence of reward"* (Hebrews 10:35).

    To have confidence is to know who **YOU** are. This alone is what will set you apart from good and great. There was a time when I knew nothing of my destiny. There was a time when my confidence was not confident and in this time I became stagnant. Allowing myself to become stagnant not only hindered me in many areas of my life but also, set me up for spiritual attack by low self-esteem. When you are dealing with low self-esteem it affects you greatly and will cause negative things to attach themselves to you.

    Self-esteem is important in growing and without it you are only blowing steam. Steam is vapor and vapor cannot be seen, so that means you are allowing yourself to be invisible. If you are invisible, how will people know the goods you have to offer another or on a greater scale, the world? Instead of choosing non-existence try transparency. Being transparent is allowing people to see through you. That means you are bold, honest and sure footed and not afraid to show it. There is a huge difference between invisibility and transparency.

    Invisibility can become such a comfortable place but it is not a place you should allow in your life. Many times when dealing with the issue of low self-esteem we can over compensate or under compensate. Those are the two different extremes we tend to go to.

> "Unwrap yourself in God's presence, that's where you'll find yourself worth being gifted to you"

EKS

Balance is needed when dealing with this issue. You never want to do too much of being seen in a negative connotation, but also not so little that we become hidden treasure. Stand up and stand out amongst those who choose to be mundane around you.

Transparency can be tricky for the fact that one might think I mean wear your heart on your sleeve or be rude and nasty towards people. That is not what I mean at all. One of the definitions of transparent is: having thoughts, feelings, or motives that are easily perceived. Being able to understand and get a grip on your emotions is critical for self-esteem to begin to rise inside you. Also, knowing how to directly express how you feel to others will truly help you in not being a victim of low self-esteem. This will help you learn to stand out and not be effected by this issue.

To be able to stand out in a world full of ordinary you have to be extraordinary. To be extraordinary is easy; just give yourself extra…extra patience, extra time and extra credit. Learn to love yourself through patience; there is a saying that patience is a virtue. To be virtuous is to have a particular excellent moral. I have been taught to do everything in excellence. Therefore, just set a standard for yourself and don't move from it.

The word of God says to let patience have its perfect work in you. You have to be patient with yourself. Celebrate the small things. You smiled more today than you have in awhile. You dressed up today and felt good about yourself. You haven't had as many negative thoughts this week compared to last. These may seem small, but it is still improvement. The smallest victory is still you winning!

Give yourself time to be molded into who God says that you are: it is stated in the Bible *"But now, O Lord, thou art our father;*

we are the clay, and thou our potter; and we all are the work of thy hand "(Isaiah 64:8). Therefore, we need not be eager to create the image we see, for we were made in His image and likeness.

Trust me, He likes what He has created inside of you; for you are a portrait of his beauty. It takes time to make a delicious meal. You have to prep the food, you have to put it together and then it takes time to bake. You have to go through process, so try different things with makeup, hair styles etc. and you will begin to see the beauty that you are!

You have to as well give yourself extra credit. Just like school teachers will give students extra work to help boost their grades, you have to do the same thing with confidence. When you seem low down, stop and do something that will boost yourself esteem. In this book I will help you with this process; I will give you tidbits of encouragement and share an important part of my personal story. I will give you prayers to pray, encouraging poetry and a healing part in each chapter to promote motivation in believing in your beauty and ultimately resulting in your total belief in YOU! The Bible tells us in Psalms that we are fearfully and wonderfully made: marvelous are thy works!

For much of my early teenage and young adult years I struggled with low self-esteem. I just could not seem to get a grip on loving me. I saw myself how other peers or negative people saw me. I devalued my self-worth. I continually marked myself down and wondered why I was always attracting bargain shoppers into my life. My belief in me was at an all-time low and because of this I could not move forward.

The Bible says faith without works is dead. I was in an even worse state then, because I had no faith and no works. Every dream

FINDING ME IN THE MESS

I would dream would be matched by negative thoughts. I was all over the place in my life. Doing way too much and not being able to get started because I had no decision making skills. Or I would believe so little that my motivation was motionless.

I was affected deeply by this issue to the point that my very nature was shifted. It is very easy to go from being a happy, optimistic, people person to being a depressed and isolated pessimist. I knew how to hide it well and because of all these different emotions, I became an emotional wreck. I had no idea how to get a handle on my emotions and was easily led astray. I dealt with many flesh issues and heart issues because of having low self-esteem.

I had many long nights of crying myself to sleep behind broken hearts. I had trust issues embedded so deep I was okay to turn a blind eye to a man cheating on me. My mind was so distorted that I was easily manipulated. My need for acceptance so strong, that I allowed myself to be controlled by others. And my desire for love had me looking in all the wrong places.

I quickly lost myself just to be found. Yet, the finding was never positive. It was like I was trapped inside one of those lost and found boxes in the back corner. Gazed at and maybe picked up here and there briefly but tossed to the side because I was not the thing they were looking for. I wanted to be noticed and I didn't care what type of attention I got, as long as someone was looking. This behavior rapidly spun me out of control and had me dealing with things a young woman should never have to deal with.

I was trying to fight off spirits I didn't even know were attached to me. Trying to maintain what was completely out of control. I was constantly smiling when I wanted to cry. My mask became a permanent fixture on my face. I had truly become a victim of low self-esteem.In this book I am going to take you on a journey. I will show you the problem and then help you to find the solution. We will travel through some of the strongest spirits that couple themselves with low self-esteem. I will dissect these issues with you and give you a complete understanding as to what they are and what they try to do. Then I will help you in finding a way to come out of their grasp and ultimately find healing. My goal through this book is to draw out the issue and give you the tools to correct it.

I pray every woman who reads this walks away knowing she is more than what she initially believed. I pray that it reaches into the depth of you and strikes a chord so deep that you never can be the same again. May this book help you to grow, to overcome and to fruitfully prosper in every area of your life! May it give you the strength to let go of the self-abuse and the complacency. You are truly more than a conqueror.

Finding ME in the MEss, will find you inside of your mess and pull you up out of the dirt. Women it is time that you wipe yourselves off and shine forth. Shine bright like the diamond God called you to be. *You are the light of the world* (Matthew 5:14), let your light shine for all to see. You can find yourself because I did. It may take time but it surely is attainable if you only first believe.

CHAPTER 1

How Having Low Self-esteem Affects You

We live in a world where as a woman all we see are magazines, movies and videos portraying what society thinks a woman should look like. If for some reason you don't meet their standard, then you are labeled "not good enough". It seems you are constantly fighting to become what is beautiful to the world. You want to feel and look the part. You want someone to notice that you are lovely.

Here's the problem with that: no one can see that you are beautiful because you look like everyone else. It is okay to be beautiful in your own eyes. There is a quote I love. It says, "Beauty is in the eye of the beholder." Therefore, the perception of beauty is subjective. If you cannot behold your own beauty first, how do you expect anyone else to? You should know you are beautiful despite what anyone else thinks. If you are sure of yourself, then others will not be able to affect your own thoughts toward you.

So, before we can understand the problems that this condition brings, we first must understand what low self-esteem is. Self-esteem is a feeling of having respect for yourself and your abilities.

Therefore, low self-esteem would be the exact opposite; having no respect for yourself or your abilities. You would always think "I am not good enough". In dealing with low self-esteem your belief in you would be the main issue.

There is the age old question, do you believe? The Bible says if you have faith as small as a mustard seed that nothing will be impossible to you. If you believe in yourself the hurdles of life won't be so hard to jump. You can move mountains with just a little faith. Situations may arise that seem huge, out of reach or defeating but having belief in yourself will cause you to triumph every single time.

I love the way Dosomething.org defined low self-esteem. They said low self-esteem is a thinking disorder in which an individual view him/herself as inadequate, unlovable, and or incompetent. Once formed, this negative view permeates every thought, producing faulty assumptions and ongoing self-defeating behavior. This allows us to know that this is a mental disorder. If you can change your way of thinking, you will change the way your life is being orchestrated.

To help you along the path of healing your mind I want to give you this scripture. *"Casting down imaginations and every high thing that exalteth itself against the knowledge of God, and bringing into captivity every thought to the obedience of Christ"* (2 Corinthians 10:5). So, any voice that is telling you that you are not good enough, not pretty enough, not smart enough, has got to go. When those thoughts play in your head you must throw them from your mind. Do not allow negativity to impregnate your mind with garbage. You are more than those thoughts want you to believe and you have the power and authority in Christ Jesus to hold those thoughts captive and to release love and peace inside of you.

Now, that I have told you what low self-esteem is, let's talk about what it does. As I previously mentioned, it is a mind disorder, so it attacks your thinking. It will cause you to become self-conscious in your looks, your appearance and your abilities. It becomes that voice inside your head that breeds negativity into you. It can quickly steal your dreams, kill your motivation and easily destroy your life.

The Bible tells me *"the thief cometh not, but to steal, and to kill, and to destroy: I am come that they might have life, and that they might have it more abundantly"* (John 10:10). Therefore, low self-esteem is of the devil because the end goal is the same. He will use whatever method he can to ultimately destroy you. Self-esteem has been an easy tactic to use and he is taking advantage of the opportunity when presented.

Your life was designed to be filled with the abundance of life. Abundance is a large amount of something, an ample quantity. Your life should be filled with huge amounts of success and a lot of happiness. You should be smiling and enjoying life to the fullest. If you are down more than you are up, then you may be dealing with a form of low self-esteem.

Low self-esteem presents itself in many forms and fashions. As I mentioned earlier, we can go from one extreme to the next or land somewhere in between. If we aren't over compensating, we may be under compensating or maybe just **BEING** and that as well is a problem. If you are just going day to day that is still not the abundant life Jesus came to give to you. If you are just going through the motions, you need to take a deep look within you and see if low self-esteem is affecting you in any way.

In dealing with your mentality, you must be strategic. You have to constantly barricade your thinking and guard your mind. It is very important to not let any and everything permeate your mind or cloud your thinking. Since low self-esteem affects the mind it will teach you low thinking. Anything you entertain will become your teacher. Therefore, be careful what school you are learning from.

Low self-esteem can easily affect you and infect you. Once you have allowed it access, it will quickly spread through your mind like a cancer. It will begin to infect every positive thought you hold. It will pollute your mind with disgust for yourself. It will even begin to cause you to become sick in your body. Once your thinking is infected it will seep out into every area of your life and slowly inflect its bite into those areas as well.

The enemy has strategically planted things all around you to cause you to lose focus on the important things and push you to concentrating on the things that matter least. There was a time you loved you. Once upon a time you saw that you were beautiful but the enemy came in through the room you made for him, i.e. that moment where someone said you looked like you gained some weight. As soon as that door was opened and you began to inspect your body for flaws; that is when he slid that negative thought in. He knew once he got that opportune time, that he would have the upper hand.

One simple comment can change us in a moment's notice. That is why you must guard your heart, mind and spirit. This is why it is important that you first love and accept yourself. With you loving you the vibes you send out will demand that same treatment. If you accept yourself, it will never matter to you that someone else doesn't.

Once you form thoughts that are positive and continually flood your mind with goodness there will be no bad thing that can prosper. You will get respect because everything about you will demand respect. When you hold your head up high you can see in front of you. You will be sure of where you are heading. The enemy's job is to get you to walk with your head down and your spirit defeated, so that you will be lost and never gain the victory.

Since the mind is a terrible thing to waste, fill it up with the good things of life. If you fill your mind with nonsense you will live nonsense. That is why you must fill it up with knowledge and then you will live wisely. The word of God says out of the abundance of the heart the mouth speaketh. That tells me that what you think enters your heart and it becomes a permanent fixture there causing you to speak those negative things.

Once you have spoken negatively it is sent to come to pass. *"Death and life are in the power of the tongue: they that love it shall eat the fruit thereof"* (Proverbs 18:21). Therefore, speaking death will manifest that form of fruit for you to chew up and swallow. There is so much power in your tongue and it can cause you to gain or to lose. What fruit are you bearing?

Low self-esteem causes you to speak death. It will only influence you negatively. On the brightest day this disease will cause you to see rain clouds on the horizon, even when there is none. You will constantly be battling with so many spirits that because of the weak state of your mind they will gain entry. Not only will they gain entry, they will take you over. You will then be so full of negativity that you no longer see an issue in your behavior.

When the enemy has succeeded in you not seeing anything wrong with your behavior, that is when Satan has truly gotten full control of your mind. You now have a condition that has become a habit. A habit takes about 30 days to fully form. Once you have made a habit of being negative and acting out negatively it is then considered a habitual behavior. The effects of having low self-esteem are truly detrimental.

Here's a story for you...

Let me tell you how low self-esteem easily crept inside my mind. I was born with a very rare bone disease. This disease quickly altered my physical appearance at the young age of one. My mother began to notice bumps forming on the joints of some of my fingers. They looked like calcium deposits or arthritis in older people where their bones disfigure and increase in size. She took me to an orthopedic doctor only for them to find that these bumps were in several places. The doctors noticed that they were inside my skeleton pretty much all over but only would appear outwardly on certain joints of my body.

They were very ugly and very painful but the disease was so rare that the doctor couldn't give us much information. As I grew these bumps grew. I was quite embarrassed by them because of course people made fun of me. My parents tried to shelter me because of this and they became a crutch for me in a sense. I was always pretty tough and brave when I was in Elementary school. Middle school was a little tougher for me but I still faired pretty well.

    I noticed by the time Middle school came along that obviously I was quite different than most people and it was sometimes a hard pill to swallow. By this time my right index finger was so bumpy and disfigured that it was extremely noticeable and people would stare. I could easily see the disgust on their face as they wondered if it was contagious. I felt like I had a bubonic plague or something. This disease had attacked me and I had no control over it but I was being treated like I asked for it.

    I became a little self-conscious and began to pull my right hand up into my sleeve. I would walk around with my hand covered by my jacket, so that means that I always had a jacket on; winter, summer, spring or fall. This called more attention to me and made me feel even more out of place. I stopped painting my fingernails with any color and only wore clear nail polish. Any way that I could be less conspicuous I went for it.

    By the time I entered high school I was very uncomfortable in my body. I felt unattractive, dorky and disfigured. I was not comfortable in my own skin. I wanted a way of escape because people were constantly making fun of me. This is just the beginning of my story…

TO BE CONTINUED…

(Healing)

BEAUTY FOR ASHES

"To appoint unto them that mourn in Zion, to give unto them beauty for ashes, the oil of joy for mourning, the garment of praise for the spirit of heaviness; that they might be called trees of righteousness, the planting of the Lord, that he might be glorified" **(Isaiah 61:3).**

The Bible says to appoint unto them that mourn in Zion, to give unto them **beauty for ashes**. If you are in a place of negativity this book is for you. God is going to take what was burnt up and turned to ash, what you thought that you lost, your dreams that caught on fire and changed to ash in your hands and make it all beautiful! Unto in this form is a variant of too and too is defined as to an excessive extent or degree. Another definition is beyond what is desirable, fitting or right.

Therefore, God is going to give unto you; beauty, meaning no matter what if you believe He will give it to you excessively! Even if it is not fitting or right, He is still going to do it! His word says that He will give you the desires of your heart, so if you desire beauty in whatever aspect of your life He will give it to you beyond what you desire. *" Now, unto him that is able to do exceeding abundantly above all that we ask or think, according to the power that worketh in us"* (Ephesians 3:20). Only Jesus Christ could love us so much to take our ash and exchange it for his beauty.

To go off the text I last quoted from the Bible in Ephesians God can do it but not only can He, He is able to do **ABOVE** what we ask or even think. Our thoughts aren't even on a level of His supernatural ability. Ashes are the residue of matter that remains after burning. It is suggestive of death. Ashes are as well defined as anything; as an act, gesture, speech, or feeling that is symbolic of regret, remorse or penance.

If you are allowing yourself to sit as ash because of something negative in your life, then you are allowing death to manifest itself upon you. You have to believe that you are more than your situation and work to improve yourself. Don't let your problems burn so long inside you that you end up with second and third degree heart burns. You do not want to just keep it bottled up because a fire, untamed, can completely burn out of control. Learn to have a cooling agent, something that helps calm you down, a way to keep your heart fire proof.

Besides your mind, your heart is the next place of greatest attack. If the enemy can get your heart weighed down, then he is able to enter into that area of weakness. A damaged heart is not going to beat properly. When your heart is not beating properly you are liable to be off rhythm in all areas of your life. A broken heart leaves you broken, an angry heart leaves you wanting revenge and a sad heart leaves you bitter. All of those things are negative and will leave you jacked up inside as well as outwardly.

What you have to do is always find the good inside the bad. Remember that every story has a moral and every problem has a solution. Never let life beat you down where you are left scarred for all of your life because nothing is ever worth holding a grudge. Holding onto negativity begins to affect your beauty. It causes aging from worry, dark circles from stress, loss of hair from tiredness. Inside it causes depression, rage and sickness. I always try to live by the quote "just live, love, and laugh and let go." You will be better for it in every area of your life, so count it all joy.

Your beauty is all your own, it only matters what you think of yourself. What is the point in trying to live up to other people's standards? There is this saying "if you don't stand up for something, you will fall for anything." This quote is very true because if you do not know who you are first you will listen to everyone's opinions of how and who they think you should be. Then you will become a part of the status quo.

According to dosomething.org it states that 44% of teenage girls are attempting to lose weight. Over 70% of girls age 15 to 17 avoid normal daily activities, such as attending school when they feel bad about their looks. 75% of girls with low self-esteem reported engaging in negative activities like cutting, bullying, smoking, drinking or disordered eating. The last percentage shows us that there may be only 25% of girls that have high self-esteem. This is an epidemic and quite sad.

Most times these negative behaviors are developed behind the thoughts and ideologies of others. No one should look down on themselves in any way but especially not to the point of destructiveness. It is one thing to grow and improve but it is a whole other thing to have pure un-love to one's own self. You cannot grow what you find is dead. We must be alive and well to grow.

One thing I want you to know is that if you are someone who is dealing with this and you have begun to dislike yourself, it is ok. There is still time to turn this around. When a seed is planted it is covered by dirt and mud. It sits in a dark place, a cold place and waits. Though it takes time, patience and care, that seed eventually begins to transform. Out of that small seed pops new life. The life is so great inside it can't stay covered and it bursts out of that secret place and grows into everything that God designed it to be.

Be thankful for that hidden place because in it God is preparing you to become greater. Where you are right now being but for a moment. *"Weeping may endure for a night, but joy cometh in the morning"* (Psalm 30:5). Your morning is coming and when you break forth like the dawning of a new day, God will get all the glory. You are truly more than what you believe and there is greatness inside of you. All that you are will come into fruition in due season.

Beauty Tips

Hair can sometimes be quite tricky. It seems that your hair can at times have a mind all its own. Hair is a woman's crown of glory. Therefore, we need to take care of it. Here are some beauty tips concerning your hair.

~ALWAYS see a professional for any color service, NEVER USE BOX COLOR.

~Invest in a great higher quality shampoo and conditioner. These are your foundation for general hair health, and your style.

~Always rinse out your conditioner with cold water, as cold as you can stand. This will close the cuticle on your hair shaft. Allowing your hair to stay moisturized longer, and prevent your hair color from fading as much.

A Simple Prayer

Here is a prayer you can pray over yourself to help you strengthen your mind.

Lord God, I thank you for who you are and I ask you to please help me to not be caught up in what everyone else thinks of me but allow me to only care what you think of me. For Lord, your word says that your thoughts towards me are good and not of evil. They are thoughts that will bring me to a good and purposed end. So, I thank you for looking out for me Jesus. I thank you for having kind intentions toward me. I pray, God that you will help to change my way of thinking and cause me to produce thoughts of good like yours are toward me. I pray in the name of Jesus that my mind be stayed in you Christ all the days of my life. I barricade my mind from negativity and anything that is not like you I command it to leave in the mighty name of Jesus. I cast down every imagination and every high thing that exalts itself against the knowledge of God and I bring into captivity every thought into the obedience of Christ. Lord, thank you for your love everlasting and I ask that your love courses through me and fills me up with a love overflowing.

In Jesus name, Amen.

Chapter 2

Stop Objectifying Yourself

Self-objectification, have you ever heard of that term? If you are wondering what objectification is let me define it for you. Objectification is defined to treat as an object or cause to have objective reality. That means that self-objectification is you looking at yourself as an object rather than a person. I like the way MizFitdefined it: it's seeing yourself through someone else's eyes and allowing that to color your perspective on yourself.

There are so many ways you can become self-objectifying. You can perceive yourself through society's eyes, other female's eyes and of course through how a man views you. All of these are bad habits to pick up and need to be filtered out of your system. You should never allow someone to color inside your lines. Your picture is already beautiful the way it has been illustrated.

Society has a way of objectifying women so much so that it's all we see day to day. You turn on the television and there are skinny, dolled up, half dressed women on every channel. As a young woman your mind sadly becomes infected by all that until your perception becomes off. Then if not corrected you take those perceptions into adulthood and walk around unsure and mentally incapable of knowing who you are. That is why it is crucial to destroy those negative thoughts as soon as they try to show up.

Society prescribes poison like doctors prescribe medication. Yet, this medicine is deadly or at least life altering. It so bad that society has strongly impacted women's perceptions so much that it affects the way we interact with one another. I see so many women hating on one another that it is quite baffling. Yet, I know that society is a huge cause for this negativity amongst women.

There was an actual story my husband read to me the other day where women were talking badly about this famous person because she wasn't revealing enough. Please tell me why a woman being modest and covered up is a bad thing again? This thought process is widely the same amongst women around the world. You are not beautiful if you are natural or aren't wearing little to nothing. As women you have to learn to uplift one another and stop turning each other into an object first and a person second.

Then, unfortunately there are the men who objectify women. They, too, have been affected by society's views on women. Their idea of a woman is normally a beautiful, skinny half-dressed model type. They see these women on television and believe it to be real life. That is where objective reality comes into play.

Just like a fairytale makes little girls believe that life will send them their prince charming and that they will live happily ever after, society can cause a little boy to believe that what is portrayed on T.V. is real life. Then, sadly, women become the objectification behind that rose colored reality and are sometimes used and abused because of that tainted idea. Women, never view yourself through anyone else's eyes but your own. An object is a thing that you can see and touch that is NOT alive. You, beautiful lady, are very much alive, therefore you're not an object. Please ladies, stop objectifying yourself; for you are simply amazing.

Objectification can do more harm than good. I know you might be wondering why it would even matter that someone does this. I will share with you why this very simple thing is not so simple at all. According to new research published by Psychological Science, "women who live in a culture in which they are objectified by others may in turn begin to objectify themselves. This kind of self-objectification may reduce women's involvement in social activism".

Since there are considerably more women than men in the world if the enemy can get inside a woman's mentality and destroy her through that said mentality, then he has succeeded in possibly ruining the chance of a strong and consistent social change. We should all be an activist in some form or fashion but if you cannot even change your mind, how can you hope to change a city, region or state? The enemy has plotted ways to corrupt a woman's way of thinking, so you won't think change is even possible. Allowing things that aren't right to just be should never be an option. Losing your voice is losing the war and the Bible says that victory has already overcome the world. Therefore, speak up and speak out.

Allowing objectification to become the norm to you is disastrous because it can cause your perception to constantly be off. If your ability to notice something easily becomes skewed, then observation will become uncommon to you. Without observation your capacity for comprehension becomes altered and that is when you become complacent. Observing things keeps your senses alert, keeps your mind moving and allows you to be on guard.

Comprehension helps you to understand what you just observed and causes you to act appropriately to that observation.

Being complacent is something you never want to become. It will cause you to become self-satisfied and you will be satisfied with unawareness, dangers and deficiencies. Coming into agreement with these things is like signing yourself a death sentence. It will cause you to become unaware of the things going on around you, whether they are good or bad. Then dangers could easily seek you out and you wouldn't even notice them. You would be deficient in many areas of your life and you would not care because you wouldn't even pay attention to the fact that they were there.

When your perception is off, then your self-perception is off as well. Self-perception is how you see yourself. i.word.com defines it as the idea that you have about the kind of person you are. If you are not observant and have become complacent, then please tell me how you would more than likely view yourself? It wouldn't be too good probably. You would possibly disregard yourself and maybe speak down about yourself.

When you view yourself in that fashion you begin to attract what you are. This is the worst part of objectification. It will cause you to be attracted to men that will value your worth as an object. You may become a trophy wife or a booty call. Because you have become used to being used, that is all that will come out of everything you do. People will take advantage of your complacent behavior and seek you out to get what they can from you. You must strengthen your mind and know your worth.

Objectification is a bad concept to have. It can cause so much worse than it can cause good. That is why it is important to keep an open mind and allow healthy relationships to be built around you. You have to have a good support system in place and allow positivity to flow. The more positive vibes you create, the more optimistic you will become.

You should see yourself as a reflection of beauty. When you look at yourself you should smile and be pleased. Are there things you might want to change? Sure! Yet, it shouldn't be that you are unsatisfied with every part of you. Mostly you should be happy about how far you have already come and look forward to where you are going.

There should be an excitement about life inside you. You should have a hope for the future and a satisfaction in the present. Each day you should be working towards your goals and accomplishing them as you go along. There should be some type of drive inside of you, that pushes you and propels you further. Life is supposed to be filled with expectation and dreams of vivid color.

Your days should not be weary and burdensome. Your life should not be full of regrets and bitterness from the past. Having that type of attitude will quickly ruin your future. You will walk into your next chapter and intertwine the storyline because you were too busy holding on to past mistakes. Life is progression; you too must learn how to progress.

You have to look ahead and move forward. There is nothing that God can't fix. Looking back will only keep you from walking into the promises of your tomorrow. Disobeying God will preserve you in the very place you were supposed to move on from. God told Lot and his family to leave Sodom and Gomorrah and not to look back. Lot and his daughters obeyed but his wife looked back and was turned into a pillar of salt. Do not get stuck on the past so much that you become preserved there like salt.

Do not allow all the work you have done keep you from the promises God has for you. Moses worked miracles, signs and wonders. He rescued the Israelites from Egypt and brought them to the border of the Promised Land. An eleven-day journey turned into forty years of wandering because he nevercould get past the people. The people had such an effect on his mind that he was hindered in his own progression. The very promise God made him personally was right in his reach but he never was able to grasp it. Moses was only able to see the promise but was not allowed to obtain it.

What disappointment he must have had to be so close but not close enough. All because his mind was stuck on the words others formulated. Let them say what they will, but you keep a precise picture of who you are. Do not allow the hurt and traumas, the disappointments and baggage of others chain you up inside your thoughts. *"If the Son therefore shall make you free, ye shall be free indeed"* (John 8:36). You were made free by the blood of Jesus, so run, dance…live.

More of my story…

High school came along very quickly and I was extremely nervous about going. I already was feeling too different from everyone else and I wasn't confident that I would fit in with anybody. I believe high school years are the toughest years for children because you are trying to pinpoint your identity, find your way from child to adult and somehow look the part while trying to figure it all out. Those 4 years are life changers for sure. I know mine were anyway and they, sadly, changed my life in a bad way.

FINDING ME IN THE MESS

When I started ninth grade I was 15 years old. I had zero experience in life and began school very nervous. I wanted to fit in so desperately and didn't want anyone to view me as a freak because of my bumpy fingers. I stayed in a quiet place and had some friends from Middle school that I would hang around with here and there. I mostly stayed to my own business though.

As time went on, I ended up making quite a few friends. I thought I was doing ok and began to come out of my shell more and more. This was probably my first mistake, to think everything was good and that high school wasn't a place of teenagers trying to fit in and look cool. I started talking more and more and being my carefree old self again. I wasn't popular but I was not a loser it seemed, so I was happy.

All the while, the enemy was waiting for the right moment to set me up. He wanted me to feel secure and balanced before he knocked me clean off my feet. See, I was quiet and fearful at first, so he knew I would be hesitant and locked up. He couldn't have manipulated me too easily that way. That is why he made me fit in somewhat, so I would let my guard down just enough that he could slip in through the crack I created.

It was in one of my classes that I saw a guy from across the room. He was quiet and mysterious, someone that was strange and intriguing to me. Those should have been more than enough reasons to stay away. I mean I was taught the whole stranger danger concept. Yet, for some reason I just had to get to know him.

Our seats in the class got rearranged and we somehow ended up closer to each other. Coincidence? I think not. This was the first step in satan's well developed plan of destruction for me. He made it so much easier for me to develop a connection to this guy because now he wasn't just the deep guy from across the room. He was now very close to me, basically in my personal space. How smart the enemy is, when he knows the desires you seek.

The first time he spoke to me was quick and quiet but it was from that moment that I was hooked. We became friends, or what I thought a friend was supposed to be. He played the game nicely, set me up to get me trapped in his web to be devoured at his choosing. I was fresh meat to a well-seasoned player. The haunting question in the back of my mind was" had he done this to others", but I allowed my naivety to cloud my judgment too much for me to reason with the answer I already knew.

To be continued...

(Healing)

NATURAL BEAUTY

"I will praise thee; for I am fearfully and wonderfully made: marvelous are thy works; and that my soul knoweth right well" **(Psalm 139:14).**

What a powerful scripture; it seems like God thought to add this for those moments when we feel full of fear and anything but wonderful. His love for us is simply amazing and life changing. I wake up and tell myself this scripture in the mirror every morning. What this does is help me to allow God to continue to mold and transform me into what I am saying.

God created us in His image and His likeness, therefore we have to begin to understand the power in this scripture. *"And God said unto Moses I AM THAT I AM"* (Exodus 3:14), so what the Lord wants you to do in speaking this, is to speak as He would, **I AM!** The word fearfully means: in fear or in an alarming manner. Therefore, you should hold your head high at all times and walk boldly. People should be alarmed when you come into their presence not because you are rude and nasty but because you walk in confidence and authority. When you know who you are the atmosphere quickly sets and people just know you mean business.

Wonderfully! When I looked this up it blew my socks off! Wonderfully, used in this form, is used as an intensifier! What God did was intensify beauty in you through the majestic beauty that is him. Your beauty is a reflection of His beauty in human form.

Intensify means to make stronger, more intense or more marked. He marked you with a touch of His intense beauty, so once you become God's, your light becomes stronger and you just simply stand out!

The Bible says *"God created man in his own image, in the image of God created he him; male and female created he them" (*Genesis 1:27). This is good to know because this means not only are you fearfully and wonderfully made by the greatest but that you were made in His image. This means you are God's representation. Representing The Lord cannot be done in a manner of low self-confidence. God is the alpha and omega, the beginning and the end, the author and the finisher, the head and not the tail and in representing Him your head should be held high and you should walk in high regard of yourself.

You are his resemblance, so you should mirror Christ. His word is there as a blue print for you to follow. He already walked the path; all we have to do is step in the impressions He already made and choose to stay the course. *"Thy word is a lamp unto my feet and a light unto my path"* (Psalm 119:105). All you have to do is walk and keep your head up because He never allows us to walk alone in the dark, He is there with you; shinning His light to help you see. God does not have low self-esteem and neither should you.

You are naturally beautiful because God is so beautiful and if you were made in His image of course you are beautiful as well. Never second guess your beauty because if you say you are ugly, then you are basically saying God is a liar and that He is ugly. How, you may be asking… Well, first off He made you and the word tells me that in us as His creation He saw that it was very good. *"And God saw everything that he had made, and, behold, it was very good…"* (Genesis 1:31). If God can see that you are good, who has risen above his thought of you to pollute your mind into believing anything less. Then second, God created us in his likeness and I know for sure He is lovely, so if we mirror Him then there is no way we are anything other than beautiful because He is not ugly.

As a natural beauty you need nothing but the skin you are in to be beautiful. I have witnessed so many women wearing excessive makeup because they have such low self-confidence. Wearing makeup will not fix the inside of you but it will only mask the outside of you. Eventually, masks have to come off and if you can't even begin to accept you, don't expect someone else to. You have to love yourself in raw form; this means when you stand before the mirror you have to truly see **YOU**. Not only should you see you, but you should see inside you. What are you made of, what are you in pursuit of, who are you?

Do you make time to figure you out? Do you know what makes you happy? Do you know what upsets you? Before God can give you anything worth holding on to; you have to give yourself you! What do I mean by that? You have to invest in yourself. You have to get to know the **YOU** that you are and then spend time delving deeper into the **YOU** that you want to be.

This is what finding me in the mess is all about, getting to know you. Despite the situation, beyond the circumstance, it is time you forget who you used to be. The Bible says *"Forget the former things; do not dwell on the past. See, I am doing a new thing, now it springs up; do you not perceive it? I am making a way in the wilderness and streams in the wasteland.* (Isaiah 43:18-19, NIV)

The Lord was saying throw away your memories of the past; stop thinking on that old stuff because it is pollution to your soul. You are no longer that person, you have been made new. The new thing in you is leaping out of you and you can't see it? Meaning, you are still so focused on the old that you aren't able to acknowledge the good of Him that He is placing within you. The Bible tells me *"Being confident of this very thing, that He which hath begun a good work in you will perform it until the day of Jesus Christ"* (Philippians 1:6). It is easy to let Him begin but it sometimes takes a long time for Him to finish because of our own selves not surrendering to the process. While on the potter's wheel, you have to give yourself away fully, let Him mold you and make you.

The molding process is not always the most comfortable but it is necessary. Isaiah 43:19 states this ...*I am making a way in the wilderness and streams in the wasteland.* How beautiful is it to know that God is still making away for you in that wilderness place?

Though you feel stranded, deserted or lost, God is creating a path to save you from that place. Though you feel like garbage, like you have created a wasteland within yourself; Jesus has created a stream of living water to flow inside that dirty place. He has come to clean you up and purify you. Out of your belly can flow streams of living water, if you empty yourself out and let Him fill you.

Only God can make new what is old and used up to us. The quote "one man's trash is another man's treasure" has never rung more true than when placed before Jesus. He looks into us with a hope for our future and He has an expected end for us in mind. We look on ourselves with disdain and a fear to walk into the future because we are too ashamed and afraid to walk past our past. We sometimes never realize that God gave us the power to triumph over it all.

When you come to Christ and surrender you become a new creature. *"Therefore if any man be in Christ, he is a new creature: old things are passed away; behold, all things are become new"* (2 Corinthians 5:17). That is God's word, **ALL** things are made new. That means no stone is unturned in your life that He doesn't wash as white as snow. There is no dark place that His light can't shine in. When He makes you new, He makes you brand new and everything around you must change as well.

He took the canvas of you. There was paint all over you. You were filled with different colors and vast signatures. There were many kinds of styles of art imprinted onto your fibers and there may have been no corner that seemed untouched. God saw it fit to whitewash you. He erased every part of the tag they placed on you and He removed their claim to you. He washed away your sin and shame and called you new. You now have a new blank canvas for God to paint; allow Him to color you bold.

You are naturally beautiful because you are a child of God. You are pretty because He calls you daughter. Your beauty is engrained in the way you think of yourself. No thought should make you feel unpretty, no word should bring you shame. Hold fast to the way God sees you and speak beauty into yourself and in time you will see beauty flow naturally.

Beauty Tips

I always find the hardest seasons for me with my makeup are during summer and winter. I live in Florida, so during the summer it can get exceptionally hot. Many times it is hard to know what makeup to wear on your face because of the heat and humidity. We need to be pampered and prepared correctly in every occasion. Here are a few summer beauty tips for you.

~Minimal makeup in the summer is your best bet. The less you wear, the less the chance of a cakey look. We naturally sweat when we are hot, and makeup does move around some in the heat, so wear less and this will easily be avoided.

~During summer instead of foundation try a tinted moisturizer or BB cream. This will help keep from that heavy makeup feeling and allow your face to breath.

~Glow!! Yes, glow is wonderful, just don't over-due it. You want radiance not shininess. Humidity causes extra shine, so stay away from creams because you do not want look sweaty and sparkly.

A Simple Prayer

Here is a prayer that you can pray to increase your belief in your beauty inside and out.

    Lord God, I thank you for being the greatest thing in my life. Thank you for loving me the way you do. I pray, God, that you will help me to see me the way you do. Open up my eyes to the beauty you created in me. I thank you for creating me fearfully and wonderfully and for calling me marvelous. If you find me good, I have no right to think of myself as anything less. So, I speak to myself and say I am beautiful. I decree and declare that I am above and not beneath. I decree and declare that I am the head and not the tail. No longer will I minimize myself-worth but I will believe in me and cause my value in myself to sky rocket. I thank you for loving me God, even when I didn't love myself. Thank you for increasing your truth of you within me, so that I am comfortable in my beauty. I love you God.

In Jesus name, Amen.

CHAPTER 3

Are You Feeling Guilty?

Guiltiness is a sign of inadequacy. That is actually part of the definition of guilt. Guilt: feelings of culpability especially for imagined offenses or from a sense of inadequacy. When you feel inadequate, you feel that you are not good enough or that you are not enough in and of yourself. This spirit causes you to feel incapable and can quietly suppress you.

When dealing with the spirit of guilt it can play tricks on your mind. It will cause you to believe that everything is your fault. Another definition for guilt is a bad feeling caused by knowing or thinking that you have done something bad or wrong. Being guilty plus inadequacy causes total dependency on whatever you are attached to. Blaming yourself is not a good place to be in.

Guilt attaches itself to people with low self-esteem because it is easy to cause you to play the victim role with guilt. "This happened and now I feel bad, you made me cry". These are all things victims use to manipulate or over compensate. Usually you are over compensating for the guilt-trip you are on. Do not allow guilt to overtake you because it will leave you manipulated and trying to have you manipulate others.

Guilt is a permissible punishment to oneself for a crime never committed. It is like turning yourself in for a crime you never played a part in. Would you just waltz into a jail, deliberately walk into the cell, slam the door shut and lock it? No, of course you wouldn't. Well, that is what guilt does to you. Guiltiness puts you behind bars and makes everyone question your innocence.

Guilt is reflected out of you from its source, which is low self-esteem. It will reflect inside of you to illuminate your need to be accepted. Guilt is a spirit that causes you to over compensate. You allow others to cast the blame on you and you go along with it just to feel wanted. On the other hand, you cast the blame on yourself to fit in. It will have you easily thinking "oh, I'm just taking one for the team".

The spirit of guiltiness will have you believing you are doing something right. It will make you feel like you are ok because you are not blaming others but are blaming yourself. What you have to realize is that it is still unhealthy. Going around feeling guilty over everything is not normal. You cannot blame yourself for anything and everything.

It is better to feel convicted, not feel guilty. Guilt will cause you to hide the truth because you are afraid of punishment. Guilt can, as well, cause premature death because when someone feels guilty that spirit can couple itself with suicide. Also, guiltiness can cause a person to accept more abuse by making them believe it is their own fault, that they deserve what is being dealt them. Guilt is the negative emotion, where conviction is the positive one.

Conviction will only come if you truly indeed did something wrong. You can't feel convicted for something you didn't do. Conviction is defined as the act of convincing a person of error or of compelling the admission of a truth. So, conviction will spring you into action. It will compel you to tell the truth. Conviction is necessary because it keeps us honest and more willing to do what is right.

Guilt will do the complete opposite. It causes you to be inactive. It causes you to want to hide the truth. Guilt doesn't want you to be honest but to just feel at fault. That spirit wants you to punish yourself over and over again for the wrong you have done.

Guilt is like a nagging voice that never goes away. It causes you to be tormented in your own thoughts. It cast you into darkness and claims there is no way out of the deep and dark place. Guilt is not good because it doesn't produce any type of good fruit. It only causes more negative and more ways to sin.

Let's look at Judas in the Bible. In Matthew 27 it talks all about how when Judas saw Jesus condemned that he regretted it. Regret is the key word here. He felt regret not conviction. His regret caused him to act out of that emotion and the spirit of guilt will lead you astray every time.

Judas went and tried to return the silver to the priests and elders but they wouldn't receive it. He went to the offenders not the victim of the offense. He should have gone to Jesus and repented. That is what conviction does; it takes you to the source of the issue. Regret will have you looking to the wrong people or person for forgiveness.

Regret is defined as an expression of distressing emotion. To act off emotion will deliver you negative results every single time. We cannot become prone to emotionalism, where we gain a tendency to regard things emotionally. Emotions can become an indulgence to us. We must use our minds not our emotions.

Another definition of regret is sorrow aroused by circumstances beyond one's control or power to repair. This definition leaves me uneasy because in Christ He always has the power to repair. Regret/guilt will always make you feel powerless and stuck. Even if in the situation you cannot fix the breach, you yourself can be repaired and made whole just from apologizing for the wrong you have done. There should always be healing and restoration, not shame and self-reproach.

Those very things are synonyms for regret…shame, self-reproach and guilt. If you are feeling regret, shame, or self-reproach chances are you are dealing with the spirit of guilt. You must seek God and wise counsel to be delivered from that spirit. Guilt can cause you to harm yourself and inflict pain inwardly. You will begin to carry all types of baggage because of feeling guilty.

This is what happened to Judas; he felt guilty and tried to fix what he had done wrong. Yet, he went about the fixing all wrong. He went to give back the prize he won for the sin he had committed. What he needed to do was go to the person he had sinned against. Giving back the money was a kind gesture, but never saying sorry to the person he inflicted the betrayal upon is wrong.

Judas, after all was said and done, committed suicide. He took matters into his own hands and killed what he never created. Guilt had taken root in him so strong that when shame manifested he gave up. Who knows how tormented his soul had become in those moments; obviously it was bad enough that he gave up the hope of restoration. Above all things you must prevail in spite of the negative feelings that plague you.

Sadly, guilt and shame can cause you to never go and seek forgiveness. It may make you feel like you will not be forgiven. That the crime you committed was so great that you can never be forgiven. It will cause you to bring reproach upon your own self. Then once it causes you to fill bad enough it can quietly haunt you and cause you to take your life.Despite all hateful things the enemy uses, God's love never fails. Look to Him and allow His love to bring healing.

In those moments when you feel that shame or guilt rising up, you have to remind yourself that in Christ there is no condemnation. His word says *"For all have sinned, and come short of the glory of God" (*Romans 3:23). You must stop trying to carry the world on your shoulders. You have to stop holding things locked up inside and then wondering why you eventually explode with a flood of emotional lava erupting outwardly. We all make mistakes, just get up and try again until you get it right.

You have to learn how to talk it out and then follow up with walking it out. You are not always to blame; everything is not your fault. Things happen and mistakes sometimes are made but it is how you navigate the ship the next time those icebergs show up in your way. Be your own solution and solve your issues head on. If you have a problem with someone, the Bible says to go to that person and that person alone. Apologize to the person you have the offense with and watch the healing that takes place inside you. Never allow guilt to settle in your heart.

More of my story...

He and I developed past a mere school friendship; I got his number and after my initial awkward call we became even more acquainted from phone conversations. It seemed we had so much in common. We liked the same type of music and had similar ideals on life. We really had more differences than similarities, but I was naïve. He was different and older and it intrigued me. There's this saying that goes "curiosity killed the cat," which was surely describing me.

I thought of him as a breath of fresh air. He was something new and invigorating. In my mind I had hit the jackpot a young girl snagging an older guy; yes, I had done it right for sure. Not only did I feel pretty cool but he accepted me, bone disease and all. He finally won me over and I gave him my complete undivided attention.

I fell for him and I fell hard. Normally when loving someone they should catch you and not let you fall, but no, nothing broke my fall. He didn't catch me or even attempt to try and catch me. He just stood there laughing as I hit the cold hard ground of reality. I had been dreaming that this guy actually liked me and could possibly love me. The reality was that fairytales were just that; tales, and I was no princess. I was not able to wish on stupid stars or dream up a happily ever after.

Before that truth became my reality though, I was living in a dream world. His smile, his coolness and aloofness swept me away. His friendship, attention and conversation kept me coming back for more. Eventually, after months of developing a friend type of relationship, he invited me over. It was our schools Christmas break and he wanted to hang out and watch movies. He was so smooth with it, that he was even able to convince my mom over the phone that he had good intentions. She dropped me off on her way to a Church's Christmas program.

I remember how excited I was just to hang out with him. When I arrived at his house, it looked so inviting. I thought that it was cozy and I felt even more comfortable. When he opened the door he was in chill mode wearing what looked relaxed, just hang out clothes. He smiled and invited me in. He and I both waved goodbye to my mom and shut the door.

His house was quiet and I asked where everyone was. He said they had stepped out to do some Christmas shopping. I was taken aback for a minute because he told my mom that his family would be there. He smiled and I quickly calmed, I knew him, he was familiar and he would never hurt me. Besides we were friends and friends looked out for one another.

We went to his room and the television was on. We sat watching it for awhile. It was some funny Christmas movie and it had me cracking up. He had his arm around me and I felt happy. I was content in that moment, I felt like how Cinderella must have felt at that grand ball. It was like I was the bell of the ball that night, oh but midnight was soon to strike…

To be continued…

(Healing)

Complex's Complicate Complexion

~The Heart of the Matter~

"Keep thy heart with all diligence; for out of it are the issues of life" (Proverbs 4:23).

Your heart is very important to God. He always looks at the heart. This scripture is so powerful in that sense. It teaches that you must guard your heart; you must keep it. Your heart must be kept with all diligence. Diligence means attention and care.

Guard your heart or keep your heart with all diligence. So, you must guard it with care and attention. Pay attention to what it is saying to you. Don't place your heart in just anyone's care. Your heart is very important and must be protected.

Inside our bodies the heart is quite essential. The heart is the pump of the body. It receives blood from the body and the right side of the heart pumps it to the lungs. Once the lungs give oxygen back to the blood it flows through the left side of the heart into every cell in our bodies. The heart is what keeps us alive and functioning properly.

The heart is so important that it is protected not just by being inside the body but it has its own barrier surrounding it. The ribs are there as extra protection to the heart. The heart is so important that it has a body guard around it for added protection. If the body knows how important the heart is, why do we fail miserably at knowing this same thing? Our hearts are necessary, so please take care of it.

The bible says the issues of life flow out of the heart. That means that anything you're dealing with is going to affect your heart. Any problem you face will flow from your heart. When we eat wrong, get too worked up or carry stress around it can affect your heart negatively. Remember to safe guard it at all times.

Let's focus on stress for a minute. Stress truly affects your physical health. It will cause you to age quickly. There is a saying that says "stress is the new biological clock". The sad thing is this quote is very true. According to dailymail.com scientists now say that stress can make your face age by a decade. They have found that stress is the over-riding factor when it comes to the rate at which we grow older.

Stress is not a good thing and can harm your body quickly. It affects the heart and the face just to name a couple. It will take its toll slowly and silently. Stress eats away at your happiness and composure like a termite does wood. Stress gnaws on it until the foundation inside of you is unstable and crumbles all around you.

Women, sadly, are most affected by stress. We carry stress like a badge of honor, when it is actually more like a heavy burdensome travel bag. We take it with us on every flight because it is there reminding us that we need to do this and do that. It has its purpose but we have to stop dragging it around all the time. We have to unload the bag and free up some space inside of our heart.

Though men may feel stress, they handle it better than women. They just face the problem head on and then move on. We women tend to let everything build up and then wrack our brains trying to figure out the best solution. Doing all that over analyzing just sounds way too stressful; there is a better way ladies. You have to learn to prioritize and let go and let God.

God says cast your cares on me because I care for you. Why do you feel the need to carry all those bags around with you? Unpack ladies and relax. Give those issues to God; protect your heart and your skin from unnecessary aging and sickness. You hold the power to be healthy and carefree.

I want to tell you the definition of complex. It is an emotional problem that causes someone to think or worry too much about something. What are you worrying about, what has your mind running all over the place? Complexes really will complicate life. They will have you stressed out until your hair starts falling out. The stress will show up outwardly until you look like a shadow of who you used to be.

As I stated earlier, stress plays a huge role in premature aging. According to afpafitness.com stress is one of the seven most common factors in premature aging. It shows up not just in the wrinkles created by worry but in the way you carry yourself and as well in your health. Stress literally makes you sick and old. Worry kills your energy levels and changes the way you think about yourself.

Our skin and complexion are important. Clean and clear skin speaks for a good and healthy life. When you take care of your skin it will make you feel better as a whole. Your skin is a reflection of what is going on inwardly. Shine out through the skin you are in.

When stress tries to show up reject it. You do not have to allow worry to overtake you. If something is looming, causing an impending doom to hover above you, you have every right to rebuke that type of negativity. It is ok to work on what you can fix but some things are for another day. The Bible says to let tomorrow worry about itself. Therefore, you can only be concerned with today on today and tomorrow on tomorrow.

Relieve stress and worry by praying. Prayer is always comforting. It helps you when you can't help yourself. Prayer is a place that puts you at Jesus' feet and allows you to empty yourself out. When we don't know what to do, somehow God knows how to comfort us.

Another thing you can do is cry. Believe it or not crying is so healing to the soul. Crying removes toxins inside the body and places a balm over your wounds. You will always feel better after a good cry. There is a quote I like; it says "crying isn't a sign of weakness, it's a sign of having tried too hard to be strong for too long." Crying is a renewing of strength, a way to empty out and make room for the new.

One of the most healing things is laughter. The word says *"A merry heart doeth good like a medicine: but a broken spirit drieth the bones"* (Proverbs 17:22). So, laughter is likened to medicine because of its healing properties. Laugh your worries away and smile even more. Both of these things will keep you from aging and give you longer life.

My favorite thing to do is write when I need a moment to clear out my head or heart. You can do whatever it is you like to do that helps you relax. The gift God gave you will always help you. We all need ways to help us calm our nerves and regroup. You are the only person who will love you the most, so look after yourself.

Beauty Tips

As I said above our skin is so important. It reflects our beauty not just our natural outward beauty but the beauty that lies inside us as well. Our skin should be healthy and glowing. It should be full of life not dry, wrinkled or bumpy from stress. Here are a few beauty tips for taking care of different skin issues or to keep you from having skin problems.

~Your skin is your foundation for any makeup application. If your skin isn't hydrated and well moisturized, then your foundation and makeup will not go on smoothly or look smooth.

~See a licensed esthetician to diagnose your skin type, i.e. oily, dry, normal and get a facial at least every 3 months to remove impurities and deeply exfoliate the skin.

~Use a facial exfoliate at least bi-weekly to get rid of dead skin. Makeup will look better on a clean and smooth canvas.

A Simple prayer

Here is a prayer you can pray when you feel stress trying to creep up.

God, hello, it is me. I thank you for who you are and I give glory to your name. I ask, God, that you would please help me to let this worry go. I give it over to you God because I know you care for me and that this battle does not belong to me. I thank you now for the victory of beating stress. I speak to my mind and I say you are sound. I will not let stress keep me up all night worrying about things I can't fix at this time. I place all this in your hands, Lord, and I move on. I decree and declare peace to be still. Peace will be my portion and I will be happy. Stress will not invade the space of my heart and will not weaken my mind, body or soul. I thank you, God, for your love flowing in and through my heart. I am not worried and I am not stressed.

In Jesus name, Amen.

"Love yourself always, despite your mistakes and through the hardships, and you will begin to see a freedom never before known"

EKS

Chapter 4
Dealing with Depression

Depression is one of, if not the worst, spirit to deal with out of the ten I am discussing. It is a strong spirit and can truly destroy your life and ultimately take your life. In this chapter we are going to find out what depression is, what it does and how to conquer it. You do not have to be a victim to depression. You do not have to allow it to squeeze the life out of you.

Depression is defined as a serious medical condition in which a person feels very sad, hopeless and unimportant and often is unable to live in a normal way. It's a deep sadness that affects your normal way of living. You cannot function properly due to this spirit. It is so strong that it takes over your normalcy. It truly is a silent killer.

Feeling this way is deeper than a passing emotion. It is like a boa constrictor that wraps itself around you and slowly squeezes the life from your body. It starts off slow and then builds and continues to build over time. Eventually, your whole life has become one big gloom and doom fest. It can quickly devour your happiness and leave you numb to the fact that it is even happening.

Depression has different levels. It is like a crescendo, starts off slow and builds. The first stage is sadness. Sadness is normal; we have all felt a little blue before. It is when blue becomes the color you choose to paint on everything every single day for weeks or months on end that it develops beyond sadness. Sadness is a normal feeling, just be careful that you do not stay down for too long. Pick yourself up and let life move forward.

After sadness you hit depression. Depression is a habitual sadness. Every day will run into the next and those days turn to years and you are still in the same condition. Not only are you still in a downcast state but it is now your normal way of life. The things you once enjoyed no longer make you happy.

Happiness will become a thing of the past once depression enters. It strips away your smile and pastes an expressionless look across your face. You will not find joy in anything, and every color in your life will become dull. You will not go out too much, but stay home lying in bed. Your mind will be filled with guilt, hurt and possibly anger.

You curl up inside of depression and it becomes your blanket to keep your warm. The cold of life begins to nip at you until what feels like frostbite overtakes your entire being. Depression settles inside and kills any fire or vibrancy you once had. It is easy to let sadness become depression. Remember that anything that goes 30 days or longer becomes a habit.

Show sadness to the door, and when you open the door to let it out, invite a new chapter of life to enter. Yes, it will be different than how it once was, but change is a part of living. It is ok to move on, it is ok to let go. Nothing, or no one, should ever be more important than your health. You have to take care of yourself, and sadness can become very unhealthy.

The last stage is major depression. Major depression is an episode of depression characteristic of major depressive disorder. The depressive disorder is a mood disorder having a clinical course involving one or more episode of serious psychological depression. This would be considered clinical depression. This stage is where you need to be seen, by a doctor for the depression.

Major depression is when sadness turned into depression becomes helplessness, hopelessness and worthlessness. When in your mind life is pointless and useless. It is where thoughts of suicide or death plague your mind. This is the stage when you must seek out help or you could possibly hurt yourself or others. Major depression wants to be the end before the end.

According to the National Institute of Mental Health about 14.8 million adults in the United States suffer from major depression. It is estimated that by the year of 2020 major depression will be second only to Ischemic heart disease in terms of the leading causes of disability. That is alarming and needs to be corrected. We have to allow sadness to take its course and not hold onto it just because we do not want to let go of what we lost. That is why God created memories; reminisce but do not get lost there.

Depression is a serious disease and must not be taken lightly. It is a disease that will take a life and not think twice about it. Depression has a high risk of suicide. According to WebMD, for people between the ages of 10 and 24 suicide is the third leading cause of death. That is a wide range of ages, starting at age 10 and ending at 24. Life has barely begun at ten and has only just begun by the time you're twenty-four.

This spirit is one that likes to operate through mind control. It will have you thinking so much bad that good won't even be considered as an option. Once it gets its grip around you it offers you premature death. The enemy uses this spirit to cause you to abort your destiny. It will lock your mind down, decapitate your spirit man and then leave you hopeless. That is when the suicidal thoughts begin to enter, when all hope is lost.

That is why it is so important to believe in God. There is so much strength you can draw from faith. The Bible says that now faith is the substance of things hoped for and the evidence of things not seen. To have faith doesn't mean that what you hope for is tangible at that precise moment but that your belief, faith and trust are strong enough to hold you until the things you hope for become evident. Faith will improve your life and your thoughts on life.

If you are dealing with sadness or depression, you do not have to continue living with it. Sometimes we put our hope in the wrong things and wonder why nothing has changed. We have to get out of our own head sometimes and just really let go. Depression is of the enemy. Do you know that the Bible says*": no good thing will he withhold from them that walk uprightly"* (Psalm 84:11)? If you put your hope in Jesus and walk with integrity, *"surely goodness and mercy shall follow you all the days of your life"* (Psalm 23:6).

Depression cannot thrive in happiness. Darkness cannot walk with light. Therefore, when sadness comes, deal with it head on; let it have its fifteen minutes of fame. When that allotted time is over though, command it to leave. Sadness is our minds way of reflecting on the thing that was lost and it helps to bring a sort of healing to our hearts. Everything can be considered useful; you just do not want to overuse it because anything that is a need can become a crutch if we let it.

You have to be strong enough not to allow sadness to become a confidant. It cannot be the scapegoat used to explain away life. You have to rise above the want to hold onto things that are now gone away. It hurts and it takes time to heal but you have to learn to embrace the good times and not clutch at the loss of it. Happiness is allowed and life is allowed, just because you lost someone or something should not cause you to lose yourself as well.

Depression is serious and can quickly lead to lives being lost. If you feel you are dealing with depression, please seek medical help. Tell someone you trust, or if it is hard to speak, write them a letter. Please do not sit there allowing depression to overtake you. Here are some warning signs that you may be dealing with depression leading to attempted suicide.

You would have thoughts or talk of death or suicide. Death will be a main theme in your speech. You could be having visions of you trying to take you own life. You would possibly have thoughts or talk of self-harm or harm to others. Sometimes people dealing with depression/suicide can begin to inflict some type of pain upon themselves. You might notice aggressive or impulsive behavior. If any of these things are present you need to seek help immediately.

Stay around people if you feel sadness trying to linger. Laugh by watching comedy shows and humorous movies. Stay positive no matter what. Life is not over and a new day will dawn. *"For his anger endureth but a moment; in his favour is life: weeping may endure for a night, but joy cometh in the morning"* (Psalm 30:5). When night is over, do not bring your mourning into your morning. Wake up, smile *"...for the joy of the LORD is your strength"* (Nehemiah 8:10).

More of my story...

Things went from simple to complex in a matter of minutes. A simple arm around the shoulder became an invitation for a kiss and a kiss led to things I truly wasn't ready for. Yet, I liked him and I knew he had to have my best interest at heart, right? Wrong. A person cannot think about what's best for another when they are too busy only thinking about what they think is best for their self. I made a decision based off of my immature feelings.

This is why I say do not base any decision off of feeling. Feeling is the fastest way to end up lost and alone. Feelings are the very things that lead you down the road of self-destruction. Use wisdom when in these situations. Think before you act, it is really that simple.

My heart was racing from excitement but mostly from fear. I had fear of the unknown because this is not how I pictured my first time. I wanted to be married and happy. I hoped to be older and way more responsible. Yet, here I was and how could I say no?

In my mind I thought if I would have said no, he would make fun of me. I was finally being accepted at school and he, an older classmate, was interested in little old me. He liked me and wanted me around. He never made me feel plagued or different. This, in my mind, had to be the next step in our relationship.

When I was little I would dream of my wedding. I would sit thinking about my future husband. I had it all planned out, marry at age 25 after I graduated college. Wait for my husband and give my virginity to him as a wedding gift and then a couple years after we are married, get pregnant. I wanted a nice 4-bedroom house and 2 kids, max. That is how I envisioned my life what seemed way back when, but now here I sat as a 15-year-old, but truly just a little girl. I was there, dealing with emotions I never felt and definitely didn't understand.

I was very nervous because I wasn't raised this way. My father and mother always taught me right from wrong. I saw some of the things others close to me had faced and I knew better to tell the truth. The boy could tell I was uncomfortable and he stopped. He asked me had I ever done this before, I said "no". He smiled reassuringly and asked did I want some water. I said "sure" and began to feel better about the situation from that small gesture.

He came back with a cup of water and I took a sip. He then just sat down and waited till I had had enough and I handed the glass back to him. He then pulled me to sit next to him. He told me not to worry and that he would be kind and gentle. I was nervous but didn't listen to God when he gave me that uneasy feeling.

God gives us small signs that something isn't right. When you are not truly walking with God, you cannot truly hear His voice. The word says *"My sheep hear my voice, and I know them, and they follow me"* (John 10:27). I had backslid by this point. At age 12 I was on fire for God and loved Him. I was in youth group at our church and it was very beneficial but things changed by the time I was 15.

The church I attended as a child only kept a Pastor for a few years. They would bring on a Pastor for about 5 years or so max and then send them to a new church. By that point we were on our third Pastor and I knew he wouldn't be around much longer. Even our youth leader was transitioning out. Sending people in and out like that rocks the foundation of faith that a young child or teen is trying to build upon.

My loss of interest in the things of God happened about 14 ½ or so because I knew that the two people who helped me find Christ were soon to leave. I lost my way then and the enemy gladly picked up the fragmented and broken pieces. Yet, the way he put my jigsaw puzzled life back together was not a correct fit. My puzzle was out of alignment, pieces were stuck where they didn't belong and I was left looking disfigured. Just to fit in, I caused myself to be out of place.

After it was all said and done I said goodbye and he said he would call me later. I didn't hear from him the rest of our break. I was distraught and confused. When I would call there would be no answer. My heart was fractured and there was no splint that would fix that type of break.

To be continued...

(Healing)

BeYOUtiful

"Thou art all fair, my love; there is no spot in thee" **(Song of Solomon 4:7).**

First, ladies you must know that you are beYOUtiful. Not only should you know that you are but I need you to remember that always. No matter what anyone else thinks or says, your beauty is unique. Your beauty was divinely created by God and you are glorious in His sight. Feel free to flow in your beauty.

BeYOUtiful, so fill you up with beauty. I am not saying be full on yourself but be fulfilled in loving yourself. Learn to BE YOU and in learning who you are, you will begin to walk easier in your purpose. You have to have confidence. You have to first believe in yourself, before anyone else is going to believe in you.

The scripture above is beautiful; the entire book is beautiful. I wanted to focus on this scripture because this is how God sees you. The New Living Translation says it this way; *"You are altogether beautiful, my darling, beautiful in every way" (Song of Solomon 4:7, NLT).* You are beautiful in God's sight. He finds you beautiful in every single way.

What I love is how He loves us despite the flaws we see. He said there is no spot in you. Wow, the perfection of Him finds no fault in us when we are made new in Him. As I told you earlier the Bible says that *"you are a new creature: old things have passed away; behold, all things are become new"* (2 Corinthians 5:17). We do not have to find fault in ourselves over and over when God has already washed that residue away.

Let the storms of yesterday blow over. That is what storms do, they eventually end. Any damage they have left behind can be cleaned up and rebuilt. No storm is that great that new life is not birthed out of it. Storms are devastating but they are also renewing.

Noah built an ark to weather the storm that was about to hit. Sometimes when you are in the right place with God; He will share the knowledge of the storms coming. That gives you time to prepare for the battle. God never said the weapon wouldn't form, He just said it would not prosper. When tongues are rising up against you, have no worries; God will condemn it.

Though the rains fell and continued to fall, Noah was safe on the ark. It is the same for us, when the storms of life hit and the rain is pelting down we are safe in His arms. He is our refuge and strength and can keep us safe. No matter how our boats are rocked He will never let us fall in and drown in the ocean of hardships. He is the Captain of all and would never allow His crew to become shipwrecked.

As Noah stayed the course God gave him signs that the waters were reducing, *"After another forty days, Noah opened the window he had made in the boat and released a raven. The bird flew back and forth until the floodwaters on the earth had dried up. He also released a dove to see if the water had receded and it could find dry ground. But the dove could find no place to land because the water still covered the ground. So it returned to the boat, and Noah held out his hand and drew the dove back inside. After waiting another seven days, Noah released the dove again. This time the dove returned to him in the evening with a fresh olive leaf in its beak. Then Noah knew the floodwaters were almost gone. He waited another seven days and then released the dove again. This time it did not come back"* (Genesis 8:6-12, NLT). He knew then the waters had abated and life could begin again.

God will send you signs that the waters are subsiding. He will give you the strength to wait out the storm. You will see the sign of new life in your mouth. The Bible says that *"Death and life are in the power of the tongue: and they that love it shall eat the fruit thereof"* (Proverbs 18:21). New life begins with life being spoken out of your mouth.

When He causes the waters to dry up, you will walk on solid ground again. When you truly make the choice to walk out this life with Him you will have no need to return to where you were during the storm. You will be granted new life; you will find the beauty in you. That is when the flood you just endured will never return in that form. God promised that he would never flood the earth again. The Bible tells me *that the promises of God are yes and in him Amen (2 Corinthians* 1:20). He will keep you if, you choose to be kept.

Just **BE YOU**, be authentically you. You do not have to fit in and be a gingerbread man. God did not create you to be a cookie cutter. You are as unique as the snowflakes in winter. You are made to be different from everyone else around you. It is ok to go outside the norm and it is ok to love your uniqueness. Highlight your peculiarity and shine bright.

You are beautiful just the way you are. Embrace your beauty and fill yourself with love until you overflow. The happier you are with you, the less you will care what anyone else says. Some say their cup is half empty but when you see your cup as half full, that is when God will pour more into you. God will fill up what you yourself believe in.

FINDING ME IN THE MESS

It is so important to be confident and secure in you and your beauty. Do you find yourself attractive? Are you secure in your body? Can you walk with your head held high? If you answered no to any of these questions, you need to spend some time with yourself. Love yourself first and watch how easy it is to love others.

Take the time to seek beauty and try new things to help you gain confidence. Learn about makeup and begin to practice. Makeup shouldn't be forbidden or taboo to a Christian woman. It should be a way for us to express ourselves and enhance our beauty. When wearing makeup, don't overdo it but definitely try it out.

Makeup is just a tool to enhance the beauty that is already you. If you are using makeup to hide yourself, you already missed it. If you are wearing makeup to draw attention, that is the wrong motivation. If you are doing either of those things, that will not heal the pain that is inside. It will actually notify people in big neon lights that you are dealing with low self-esteem.

As well, if you feel you HAVE to wear makeup, you have it all backwards. You have now become dependent on a cover up. It is you truly hiding behind a mask and not being comfortable in your own skin. Makeup is not a necessity or at least it shouldn't be. You should be more comfortable without makeup then you are with it. As I said, makeup is made to enhance or highlight the beauty that you already are.

If God loves us enough to see the good inside of us, we should be able to do the same. Truly look for the good in you and about you and once you find it embrace it. Take your best facial attribute and showcase it. If you love your eyes, make them stand out. To make your eyes pop, use eye shadow, eye liner and/or mascara. Remember to just beYOUtiful and that will give you fulfillment in life, just loving yourself will change so much.

Beauty Tips

Winter at times can be as harsh on you as you may be on yourself. You have to do things a little different if you live somewhere where winter is prevalent. Winter does a lot of drying out of the skin and hair. Winter can have you looking super pretty if you do it right. Here are a few tips to help you look your best in the cold months.

~Winter winds are sometimes stinging, and can cause tearing of the eyes, so use water proof mascara to keep from having raccoon eyes, and water proof makeup so you won't have a tear streaked face.

~Always use a SPF on your skin because the winter sun can be just as brutal as the summer sun. A SPF 30 is always a good thing to have.

~It is important to pay attention during winter to your facial skin. You may have to switch your cleaning routine up during this time of year. Try a creamier or milkier cleanser in the winter because these have less skin stripping detergents in them.

A Simple Prayer

Here is a prayer to help you fight depression.

Lord, I thank you for being Abba in my life. Thank you for loving me and calling me your love. You love me despite my flaws and I thank you for how pure your love for me is. I ask you to heal me on the inside Lord. I ask that every dark place that is inside me, that you light it up with your marvelous light. You told me in your word that marvelous are your works and I am a part of your works. So, I thank you for my being marvelous and I speak that I begin to believe that I am marvelous. I thank you that my beauty was masterfully created by you. The time you took to mold and form me brought a smile to your face and you said I am good. I believe that I am good. I rebuke the depression that is trying to grab a hold of me and I break its effect over my life right now in the name of Jesus. I will not be a victim to the spirit of depression, so that it can take my life from me. I speak to my mind to cast down every imagination and every high thing that exalts itself against the knowledge of God. I, as well, bring every thought into the obedience of Christ. I decree and declare that the peace of God that passes all understanding will keep my heart and mind through Christ Jesus. I will not be overtaken by depression or thoughts of suicide. I send them back to the depths of Hell and I speak happiness over me. I speak the joy of The Lord to be my strength.

In Jesus name, Amen.

Chapter 5

Closed Up in Isolation

What is isolation? Isolation is defined as the state of being in a place or situation that is separate from others. It means you are by yourself. Isolation causes deliberate solitude and welcomed seclusion. It is a spirit that cuts you off from the world and the people around you.

Sometimes we think we should get away from everybody and retreat into some quiet place where no one can bother us. Yet, we tend to think it is just a separation. What we may not realize is there is a difference between separation and isolation. One helps you to refocus and take a moment to just breathe. The other leaves you feeling alone and closed off from everything.

Separation is defined as a point, line or means of division. In going through separation, you may feel sad. You may be trying to figure something out and you took some time away to clear your head. This is normal, everyone needs a moment to be in a quiet place and just let peace be still. It is when separation becomes the norm that you have crossed the line.

FINDING ME IN THE MESS

Isolation is an unhealthy separation. It is more than just division; it is when you have completely decided to be apart from people. Isolation causes a numbness to develop, where you feel nothing. It will cause you to become void of all emotion. Isolation stresses detachment from others but the withdrawal is deliberate.

The enemy hopes to get you alone and have you sitting around doing nothing. The Bible says *"Be sober, be vigilant; because your adversary the devil, as a roaring lion, walketh about, seeking whom he may devour"* (1 Peter 5:8). He wants to be able to destroy you through your emotions. He wants you to be in your feelings so deep that he can cause an offense to happen upon you. Once you are offended, your defenses go up and you back away from the situation. If this is how you handle things that arise, you are walking a thin line because you can easily hold a grudge that can push you over into isolation.

When we get angry, anger leads to separation and as I said separation can lead to isolation. We cannot choose to be an individual island because we are mad at someone or something. We need our alone time but we need people to survive at the same time. We were created to interact, not to be lonely. God even saw that when he created Adam, that he had no one like him. God seeing the effect of loneliness created someone he could talk to and be with. You can easily read this in Genesis 2:18-23.

Let's look at the prison system and see the effects of solitary confinement. According to Craig Haney, a psychologist, he has had prisoners tell him that the first time they've been given an opportunity to interact with other people, they can't do it. Haney told Front Line that the prisoners just don't come out of their cells.

They have become so used to isolation that they deliberately withdraw. They are now uncomfortable around people.

Isolation majorly affects our minds. It has been shown to increase cancer cell growth in people. Self-mutilation and suicide are greater in people who experience long bouts of loneliness due to isolation. It has been shown to drive people mad, because we were built to interact and socialize. This brings me to another area isolation can affect, our social life.

Social isolation is a lack of social interaction, contact, or communication with other people. This area of isolation really affects your relationship with your intermediate family and close friends. Isolation pulls you away from everyone who loves you and puts you in a secluded place inside yourself.

According to medicaldaily.com a study in 2013 published in the journal *Psychological Science* found social isolation increased people's likelihood of death by 26 percent, even when people didn't consider themselves lonely. As well they found that social isolation and living alone were even more devastating to a person's health than just feeling lonely. We all have dealt with loneliness in our life, and probably will again, but feeling lonely and utterly being alone are extremely different. Loneliness is made to fade. A good example of this is when a loved one passes away; you may feel lonely because you miss them. Being alone is when the feeling of loneliness has overtaken your mind to the point that it has pushed you away from everyone and caused you to isolate yourself from everything.

We, as humans, are a species that depend on one another. We thrive off of social interaction. We were not designed to be apart from each other for drawn out moments of time. We are social creatures and we need one another to be well and survive. You have to break isolation for your overall health and happiness.

Now that we know what isolation is, here are some of the ways it manifests itself and how it affects you. We now need to be told how to effectively combat this spirit. This spirit can easily lead you into depression and guilt. Spirits like to pair up with one another and isolation is one that likes to connect itself to strong spirits. It definitely defines that whole "misery loves company" saying. It brings you pain and misery and separates you from others, but it is ever so happy to have company over.

According to thriveworks.com the average family unit is severely fractured. The divorce rate is at almost 50 percent and more people live alone today than ever before in American history. A lot of people dealing with isolation have severe relationship issues. They have a lack of confidence, are dealing with depression and can be very cynical. They feel rejected, alienated and inadequate.

One of the first things we must learn to do is to communicate. Communication is key in anything, especially in healing oneself. You have to know how to communicate what you are going through. You cannot get effective help without first knowing what is causing you to have an issue. Maybe you are hurt by the way someone treated you, or you didn't understand someone's point of view. A lot of times we, as humans, tend to run with the idea we have of someone or something instead of taking the time to ask questions to better get an understanding of what the person meant.

If you can learn how to communicate openly and honestly, you would see a whole lot of things shift for the better in your life. Offense wouldn't be able to become your comforter. With offense removed it would directly impact the way your defenses build a wall around you. Once your walls are knocked down, the false protection that the enemy built would be obliterated and isolation wouldn't be able to trap you in the confines of those four walls. Communication is a good thing to begin to develop.

Another way to help you not fall into isolation is to build trusting relationships. The more trusting and strong relationships you have the better off you will be. The Bible says *"For by wise counsel thou shalt make thy war: and in multitude of counsellors there is safety"* (Proverbs 24:6). We all need at least one person who can be truthful with us and tell us "hey, you are messing up, this isn't good". We need someone who is on the outside looking in.

Relationship keeps us grounded. Having strong friendships and having stable mentors in your life will help in keeping you walk in a more correct and upright way. We all need to be accountable to somebody. I know we always say only God can judge me but we need other people to judge us as well. Judgment is not necessarily a bad thing all the time, sometimes it is a simple observation and kind reminder that you may have walked a little to the left. God does the final judgment over your life; wouldn't you want someone here on earth keeping watch over you for your soul's sake?

The last and most important thing you can do to keep from isolation is to love. Love is the most healing thing you can ever do. When you love, you are selflessly giving away you. Loving someone despite what they have said or done is the simplest way to a life free of bitterness, loneliness, strife and separation. To give love is to receive love.

The Bible says *"Above all, love each other deeply, because love covers over a multitude of sins"* (1 Peter 4:8, NIV). So, when you love someone past their condition or issue, you have just covered their sin. When you love, it lights you up inside because it shines a light on every hidden thing lurking in the corner of your heart. Love is a broom that sweeps away the dirt, debris and cobwebs that are trying to accumulate inside of you. When you love, you have removed every possibility of something negative hanging around.

Communication, relationship and love: these are the ingredients to blocking isolation and any of its friends. It will keep offense at bay because you will have that trustworthy person telling you "no, you were wrong for handling things in that manner." We all need guidance and direction. You will keep your defenses from overreacting because you feel offended by communicating with each person, so it doesn't lead to a loss of friendship. Most times we have allowed our own opinions of a situation to cloud our judgment. Adding love into the mixture is like the icing on the cake. It adds a sweetness to you that is necessary in having an abundant and fruitful life. We all need mercy, grace and love; so show others the same thing you desire to be shown toward you.

More of my story...

So, once Christmas break was over we went back to school as usual. I was so nervous and a little angry and hurt because of the lack of communication on his part. I wanted to hide from him but I wanted to confront him on it as well. By the time class had arrived I had lost my ability to confront him on any of it. I just sat down and gave him the same silent treatment he had previously given me.

FINDING ME IN THE MESS

He looked at me and laughed. He played my game for a little bit, not caring about my pouting and laughing at my angry glares. He finally asked what was the matter with me. I couldn't believe he had no idea what was wrong with me. How dare he do me wrong and not think I would be upset.

I stared at him with a blank stare and he looked right back blankly and obviously confused. I finally just stated the facts. "I am upset at you" I said, "I am mad because I gave you a piece of me that I can never get back and you haven't called me since." He smiled wickedly and said "I was super busy over the break." I really didn't like that answer, but what could I do?

For some reason I didn't quite understand I felt rejected. I felt alone in a new land that was cold and empty. I was confused and the land I had entered was covered in ice and wild winds of frost blew right through me, slicing my heart and making it bleed. I was numb and frostbite pricked at my soul. This was heartbreak and it was my first of many times feeling empty and alone. I was introduced to emotional pain through this.

Days crept by like sneaky teenagers trying not to get caught, and somehow on their slow decent the days quickly turned into weeks. Weeks then became months but the bite of coldness never left my side. I didn't comprehend what had happened. I wracked my brain over and over trying to figure out the reason. What did I do wrong, why did he no longer like me?

Somewhere in my mind I was playing the victim but the other side of me was bathing in guilt. I blamed myself one minute and the next I was crying because I wanted to be the victim in it all. I was a 15-year-old wrought too tight with emotions my young mind couldn't even begin to understand. The rawness of these feelings had me experiencing things a child could easily be destroyed by. That is exactly what happened to me too...I was blotted out. I felt destroyed by the life I was living, blotted out by the pain that was occurring. I wanted a do over.

I was now invisible and wanted to stay that way. I was hurt and wanted to lick my wounds. I felt betrayed, angry, confused, used and dependent. I wanted him to know what I felt and yet I still wanted him to notice me. I hated him but yet wanted his attention even the more. This was just the beginning of the volatile life I chose for myself. When a soul tie is created it is ever so hard to untie it...

To be continued...

(Healing)

Celebrate Your Life

"Thou wilt shew me the path of life: in thy presence is a fulness of joy; at thy right hand there are pleasures for evermore" **(Psalm 16:11).**

Life is a celebration. It is full of surprises and dreams coming true. Sometimes I find that people focus so much on the bad that good can never win. We come into agreement with negative so quickly, that the positive is overlooked and forgotten. Good can't happen because we are so full of negative that the bad in the world seems to be attracted to us.

If you would get in tune with God and live in His presence, joy would live in you. The scripture says that in His presence there's a fullness of joy. Joy is a feeling of great happiness. To be filled with joy is to be greatly happy. Who wouldn't want to be happy?

Joy comes from the Lord. The Bible says *"...Neither be ye sorry, for the joy of The Lord is your strength"* (Nehemiah 8:10). You should no longer live downcast and heavy laden but be filled with His joy. May you today be strengthened by God's joy! May joy enter your heart and fill you up with happiness.

If you allow God to He will show you the path of life. So many times we walk through something God never intended for us to go through. We walk right off the path that He made for us. His word states *"Trust in the LORD with all thine heart; and lean not unto thine own understanding"* (Proverbs 3:5). When you acknowledge Him, He keeps you headed in the right direction.

When you decide that you want to go another way, God won't stop you because He gives freewill. The enemy places what looks like short cuts along the road that God created and if your eyes are not focused on Christ those short cuts are going to be appealing to you. You may see the luster of life and go off in that direction but what you thought was shining will turn out to not be so bright after all. Because you went off the path it will take you a longer time to find your footing to even begin to look for that well beaten path. He already walked the path for you. All you have to do is step into the footprints of Jesus and you will win in life every single time.

If you stay the course and continue to walk in the direction He has shown you, there will be pleasures for evermore. What is more pleasurable than a good, happy and full life? Walk with God and He will make your life happy. Negative won't magnetize itself to you because it will repel against you. When you and God agree, the enemy becomes repulsed and cannot so easily attach anything bad to you.

"Can two walk together, except they be agreed" (Amos 3:3)? That is scripture and it is very true. When we do not agree with someone we do not hang around them. There is a saying that says "birds of a feather flock together." When you are alike to something you will stay around that very thing. You're attracted to what you are, so if you are full of happiness and joy, sadness and negativity can't stay connected to you.

Be full off of God's joy. Find happiness in Him and watch happiness find you in life. Follow in His footsteps and He will shine a light, so you will never be in darkness. *"Thy word is a lamp unto my feet and a light unto my path"* (Psalm 119:105). No darkness can dwell in His marvelous light.

The question is: how can I enjoy life? When you have programmed your mind to be accustomed to the bad things in life, you will have to deprogram your thoughts. You have to begin to speak life that you might have life. The more positive your thoughts, the more positive your living. When you can see the silver lining in the dark luminous clouds; that is when you will begin to believe that the sun was made to shine despite the rain.

Being optimistic is a good way to help change your thoughts. Not only will it help your thoughts to be more positive, it will also help you to lead a happier and healthier life. Optimism is proven to reduce stress and release joy. Find things to be optimistic about and you will see a transformation in your life overall.

According to a study at Yale University, optimists live longer than pessimists. Researchers found that when an optimistic person was confronted with a health crisis, they were more likely to recover quickly due to their willingness to adapt and actively participate in treatments. Because of their lack of hopelessness, they face less stress and less depression. Just being even moderately positive can lower a person's chances of getting heart disease. Laughter really does do a heart good, like a medicine.

The happier you are the healthier you are. They found this to be true during a study that Carnegie Mellon University did. Psychology Professor Sheldon Cohen found that happy people are less likely to get colds and flues. His conclusion was that positive emotions like optimism and self-esteem may play a role in people's resistance to being sick with common day to day illnesses. These happy feelings essentially send signals from the brain to your body's organs, strengthening immunity.

Being positive will cause you to take better care of yourself. Naturopathic medical doctor Alan Christianson explains being positive denotes healthy habits being formed in your daily life. The study showed that optimistic people, especially women, are more apt to engage in positive diet, exercise and self-care than less optimistic people. It showed that pessimists felt that they had no control over their eating or weight and therefore did not take control over the unhealthy habits they had. Biologically speaking, being active causes your body to release endorphins, which are feel good chemicals. They have the capacity to relieve stress and anxiety, causing you to be happier.

Optimism will put you in a better mood. When you are in a better mood life is altogether just better. Your thoughts have a direct effect on your emotional health. According to transformational happiness expert Elizabeth Manuel every single thought creates a biochemical reaction. Negative thoughts generate anger, fear and dread while positive thoughts produce contentment, pleasure and calmness. When you are happy it will cause others around you to be happier as well.

So, now you are probably wondering how you can be happy consistently. To be happy and wear a happy face you, have to find joy. Joy is a sustaining agent. It goes deeper than happiness can. It comes from a place deep inside of you. It is the pitcher you need to make the lemonade from the lemons life threw at you. Without joy, happiness is hard to hold.

Also, to have a happier life, you have to celebrate the small things. Understanding that the simple things in life are the greatest joys is extremely helpful. Waking up to the sun shining in through your window should bring a smile to your face. A small thing such as a hello from a stranger, a kind word or thoughtful gesture can do nothing but improve your quality of life. Remembering the small and celebrating that which is thought to be little, will only make you look forward to even greater.

Times, of course, won't always be happy and positivity doesn't always express itself through us. There may be a down day or week, but it is the point of trying to make positivity surface to the top through every obstacle in life. The more optimistic your outlook is, the more you can help undo the damage from in the past, present and in the future. Being positive will regulate negativity, so that it has little effect on you. Darkness may come, but when light hits it, the darkness must flee. Let your light of hope, happiness and optimism shine from you, so that the darkness of negativity will be forever petrified.

Life should be celebrated because life never goes out of style. Waking up every day is reason enough to celebrate. Every single day of your life is a special occasion. The Bible says *"It is of the LORD's mercies that we are not consumed, because his compassions fail not. They are new every morning: great is thy faithfulness"*(Lamentations 3:22-23). That means that with each day there is a new goodness to every situation that meets you on that new day. God is faithful!

You are alive so enjoy what life has to offer. Stop waiting for that special occasion to set your table with your fine china. Pull that china out and eat off it because you are worth it and should treat yourself to the best. Why wait for that right moment when you can live in the moment? Life is truly what you make it, so make the best out of it.

Beauty Tips

Nails are very important in how your appearance looks. When your nails are clean and manicured, it shows that you live a nice and clean life. Manicured doesn't necessarily mean that you are going to get your nails done by a professional every week. It just means that you are taking care of them and that they are neat and properly maintained. Here are a few tips for keeping your nails up to par.

~When you run out of nail polish remover, don't worry, use clear nail polish over your nails and then wipe it off, it will remove the old polish. .

~when you cannot take looking at your nail color any longer, go ahead and remove the polish to begin anew. You should limit your use of remover to once a week and use an acetone-free formula whenever possible.

~Your manicure can last longer if you apply a layer of clear nail polish over your regular nail polish every two days or so.

A Simple Prayer

Here is a simple prayer to pray to ward off isolation and to keep you celebrating life.

      Lord God, I come before you just thanking you for your love. I thank you even the more for who you are and for what you are doing inside of me. I give you praise for being everything to me and for keeping me. I thank you for the relationships you have built around me. Thank you that they are relationships that keep me positive, when I can't be positive for myself. I pray for relationships that are strengthened by honesty. Send me friends that can tell me the truth. When I go astray, let my friends show me my error, and pull me back into alignment. I thank you, God, for sending the right people into my life. Let me remain friendly, that I might make a friend. Keep me from hiding myself away from the people who care the most for me. I rebuke isolation right now in the name of Jesus. I will talk more and all together live more. I celebrate my life and I speak happiness over me. I will be happy and I will remain happy in Jesus name. No more days of seclusion and separation. I will live and flourish all the days of my life. Happiness will be my portion.

In Jesus name, Amen

Chapter 6

Pride Issue's

In this chapter I am going to talk about the spirit of pride. It probably doesn't seem fitting for it to be in a book about low self-esteem, right? Wrong, to contrary belief pride can manifest itself by many different things that are forming. Pride is a way for someone to hide what is really going on. We sometimes wear pride to mask hurt and insecurities.

Let's talk about what pride is. Pride has a few definitions, but there is one main one I want to focus on. Pride is defined as a feeling that you are more important or better than other people. I am sure you are scratching your head as to how someone who is beating themselves up would ever think they are better than anyone. It is a defense mechanism.

Pride is the quality or state of being proud. It is inordinate self-esteem; a pride that exceeds reasonable limits. Therefore, you would be doing one of the two things that come with low self-esteem… over-compensating by being proud. It is a false pride though, because inside you really feel less than worthy, but your normal dose of pride attacks you because it wants you to know your worth, so it over works itself and rises up in a negative way. We all have pride, but we have to keep it in check because once pride manifests negatively, that is when you have a problem.

If you do not have a good sense of self, the inward emotion of pride can change from the good form to the bad form. Being proud is normal; you ace your test and you feel good about yourself. That is fine and is quite normal. It is when pride becomes inflated that it is no longer normal and is going to ultimately hinder you in many, if not every, area of your life. Pride is a very complex secondary emotion, and has to be felt with extreme care.

Pride has, as well, been defined as a disagreement with the truth. You really know something is true, but you cover it up by reflecting pride. Yet, I want you to please understand that every reflection is just a mirrored image, so somewhere inside is you staring right back at you. There is a saying, "you can run but you can't hide." Run all you want, but to defeat a pride issue you have to face what you are trying to hide.

Pride is associated with guilt. Ding, ding; do you remember my speaking on that in chapter 3? You may have guilt because you feel you have failed yourself. Once guilt has been allowed in, it opens the door to pride. Remember spirits like to invite their friends over. They do not inhabit a place by themselves, they always couple themselves.

Often times when you are being gripped by low self-esteem you use pride as a vice. It becomes our moral weakness. Pride, if not dealt with swiftly, can become bad behavior and will eventually become an immoral habit. Pride is infectious and is something that makes one sit higher in their own mind than they should. The Bible says *"For I say, through the grace given unto me, to every man that is among you, not to think of himself more highly than he ought to think; but to think soberly, according as God hath dealt every man the measure of faith"* (Romans 12:3). This means be humble and stay grounded.

Pride is a heart issue and because God looks at the heart, this will affect your walk with Him. As Christians we are called to be servants first, pride will destroy servant hood. It will change your mind to "I am too good" or "you are not good enough for me to help." It is a sickness that leaves you cold and alone. Pride will cause involuntary isolation.

Lucifer had a pride issue and because of this he lost his place in heaven with God, the Bible says *"Thou was perfect in your ways from the day that thou was created, till iniquity was found in thee "*(Ezekiel 28:15). What type of iniquity was found inside Lucifer? Listen to what the Bible says: *"You became too proud because of your beauty. You ruined your wisdom because of your greatness. I threw you down to the ground. Your example taught a lesson to other kings"* (Ezekiel 28:17, NCV). The gifts and splendor he was blessed with, though great were nowhere near the AWESOMENESS that is God.

He was then thrown down from heaven to the ground. He was so proud of himself that he began to desire what did not and could not belong to him. He wanted God's position and glory; he was not satisfied within himself with what God had created. He wanted more, he wanted even better. Lucifer was dealing with self-generated pride.

When dealing with pride you become entangled in the web of satan. It is an ill-devised scheme that he will bring you into pride from low self-esteem. He wants you to fall and be condemned the same as he was. The word says *"Not a novice, lest being lifted up with pride he falls into the condemnation of the devil"* (1 Timothy 3:6). Pride will cause you to fall into the same disapproval as satan.

Pride causes you to lose your place in worship of God because you begin to worship yourself. The first of the Ten Commandments states "put no other gods before me." Pride is a form of idol worship. When you worship yourself you slip into the same mind set as satan and look at yourself as God (or a god). We were created to give worship to God; pride is the worship of self.

When we improperly estimate our sense of self-worth, rather it be exaggerated or minimized, we have opened the door for pride to dwell in us. Sadly, a lot of times when you are affected by low self-esteem you get the symptom of pride. Pride will cause you, when you feel low, to try and speak highly about yourself. Usually by bragging or exhibiting arrogance, you will cause pride to attach itself to you. Pride can only enter if you set yourself up to allow it to.

You must always be honest in your evaluation of yourself. The Bible says to measure yourself by the faith God has given you. You have to learn to have sound judgment of yourself. Try to see you the way God sees you. If you have faith in the creator, then you will have faith in what He the creator created. You are His creation and you should be able to be satisfied within yourself.

The Bible teaches to leave no room for the enemy. If low self-esteem has etched itself inside your heart and mind begin to lean on the scriptures of The Lord and apply them to your wounded ego. If you do not protect yourself, pride can become a hungry monster that will feed off your weakness. It is like a cancer; it just keeps growing and growing. Pride truly does come before the fall. This spirit was the beginning of destruction for all creation. Be careful to not allow it to destroy you.

To get a handle on pride you must first get a handle on yourself. We tend, as humans, to journey between these two extremes, either thinking too highly or too lowly of ourselves. The truest opinion of oneself should only be based on what God says that you are. You have to begin to see yourself as God sees you. Find your perfect balance in Christ because you are in Christ Jesus and He will keep you in right standing.

Who you are, and how you act, is a reflection of your relationship with the Holy Spirit. The more time you spend in prayer, studying the Bible and in worship, the more you will be in tune to His song. He will keep you in harmony and everything will be blended and balanced within you. God will give you perfect pitch and you will be able to recreate his musical notes without a reference tone because you rely entirely on God. If your song is full of Him, you will never have an empty place to fill up with you.

If you stay in the place of constantly growing close to God, you won't have the issue of finding validation from anyone else. You will be confident in who you are because of who's you are. Esteem will not become a conflict because you are weighing your value on the price that Christ already paid for you. Pride, as well, will not become an issue because you should be continuously searching yourself for ways to be more Christ like. Being filled with God will keep you from many snares of the enemy.

Pride is a self-fulfilled issue, and it attacks the ego causing it to seem puffed up. If you love yourself enough but always leave room for growth, you will be harder to fill with pride. Allow love to be poured into you and to flow out of you and pride will have no solid ground to stand on. Being how God wants you to be and living as an example of Him will cause God's standard to come in like a flood every time. The enemy can try to come in but he will lose his footing and be swept away by the flood of The Lord.

More of my story...

As time went on he moved right along but I never could. I was stuck in limbo and couldn't seem to push myself back upright. My ego was wounded and I wouldn't let the wound heal. Every time I could have possibly let go and allowed time to be my Neosporin, I overly determined, picked at the scab until it once again bled. Constantly replaying that night inside of my mind screwed up my thinking.

I became dependent on memories of the fake happiness we had before he won the prize that it seemed he was after. I just wouldn't allow myself to believe the truth that stood right there in front of me. It was there in plain sight; he had used me. Like most people do when a big blue elephant is standing in the room, we just simply ignore it. I went around it and acted like it wasn't even there.

Eventually, truth has a way of catching up to you. Somehow that elephant made me notice it and the truth is it did nothing but anger me. I went from a place of numbness to a state of anger. I was so mad and furious that I plotted ways to make him pay. I thought things like "I will date his close friends" or "I will lead him on and leave him messed up and wanting me." These ways of thinking were just immature and destructive thoughts, which would have only ended up hurting me in the long run. There was a monster that had been created within me and it wanted out to wreak havoc on everything and everybody.

    I began to obsess over my appearance. I wanted him to see me, not really me inside, but my body outside. I wanted him to know he had messed up and had missed out on what he could have had with me. I began wearing tighter clothes, shorter skirts and shorts. I wore things that made people look at me more, but it was negative attention. I was literally flashing a light on myself, displaying my goods at the front window of my store. I was basically saying "this is what I have to offer, come on and try it out".

    I was getting all kinds of male attention, but I was completely out of my element and I was so uncomfortable. This wasn't me, that girl that pretended she was better than everyone else was not me. The pretending to be better than others was just a mask to hide the pain and awkwardness of my feeling self-conscious. I hated the person I was becoming but I had lost myself along the way and my confidence was off balance. I became a breeding ground for negativity to form and fester. It found me when I was most vulnerable and took advantage of me in my time of weakness.

    I became a girl warped. My thoughts on reality were warped. My actions, because of my misconceived thoughts, were warped. I was just walking in some type of twilight zone like I was a zombie. This behavior became the norm to me, it made sense to me. It was a cocoon of protection and I told myself I will emerge from this as a butterfly…wrong, I emerged as a broken vessel that wanted everyone else broken too.

    Because I was so self-conscious and hurt by someone I had trusted, I began to trust nobody and flaunt my body. The way I was acting attracted guys to me. Like a moth to a flame they came to me.

It felt good, but it was a false sense of admiration and it eventually became my crutch. I used my body to fill the void of love I so desperately wanted and needed. My home life played a huge role in my behavior as well; we will get more into that shortly.

To be continued...

(Healing)

Boosting Not Boasting

***"When pride cometh, then cometh shame: but with the lowly is wisdom"* (Proverbs 11:2).**

Pride is a spirit that brings shame with it. A lot of times pride enters because of shame. These two spirits work hand and hand. When shame has entered into you, your defense is to make you feel better about yourself. It is not normal to think of yourself negatively, and your mind tries to defend you.

The problem is that when you began to think highly of yourself, because of your now wounded spirit, you fill yourself up too much with better. You have to make yourself believe you are better because you were shamed somehow. Shame is one that will cause pride to happen quickly. Shame is made to make you believe that an embarrassment will never go away. Having shame makes you uncomfortable in your own skin.

Once you feel uncomfortable inside yourself, that is when pride attempts to make its entrance. Pride comes as a result of not allowing mistakes to be learning experiences. When mistakes are made, you should grow from them, but sometimes you want to pretend that it never happened. You cause yourself to believe that mistakes shouldn't happen to you because you are better than that. When you have even that simple thought, it is enough to give room to pride.

Pride is the type of spirit that will blow you up just to deflate you. It is a spirit that will sit you up just to make you fall. This spirit once attached will make you a believer of self so much that you may become self-centered and self-ambitious. You will think only of yourself and what is best for you. The problem in that is that everybody stumbles and sometimes falls, but pride will try its best to keep you down once you have tripped.

You have to remember *"For by grace are ye saved through faith; and that not of yourselves: it is the gift of God"* (Ephesians 2:8) If it wasn't for God's grace, we all would be messed up. That is why it is so important to stay lowly with a humble and teachable spirit. God can use a vessel that will yield to Him much easier than He can a tight fisted know it all. Open up your hand and your heart and let God place His worth inside it.

There is so much wisdom in a lowly place. I do not mean that in a bad way, but truly the Bible says *"Blessed are the meek: for they shall inherit the earth"* (Matthew 5:5). Meek means humble or lowly, so in essence when you are humble God can sit you before the kings of the earth. They will look at you and see Christ because you have never allowed Him to be misrepresented. They will see His glory on your countenance.

FINDING ME IN THE MESS

Even when dealing with fires, it is said that you should get low and crawl. Hot air rises and chokes you out, this is like pride. It is so hot and puffed up that it begins to strangle you. Yet, when you stay low you can breathe easier. There will be a clearer direction where you can use discernment and wisdom. Stay humble because it is the best choice.

The scripture above states that with the lowly there is wisdom. When you stay in a place of being teachable it shows that you have wisdom. Wisdom is attained by forever learning. If you continuously are taught, you will continuously grow. Pride makes you feel that you have more than enough knowledge and cannot be taught by anyone.

To heal yourself from pride you must boost, not boast. One definition of boosting is to help or encourage. You become an encourager. To be able to help lift someone's spirit or self-worth, will in turn help you boost your own self-esteem. There is a saying, "it is a blessing to be a blessing" and this is really true. When blessing someone else it will make you feel good.

It has been proven that it takes more muscles to frown than it does to smile. That should be a great reason to keep a smile on your face. When you smile more, those around you will smile more too. It feels good when you see someone happy and perky and it is like a chain reaction. Your smile will become like a yawn, contagious, so keep smiling.

There is something called "helpers high." It is when you help another and it makes you feel good. What better way to bring about a good mood than helping another? Connect with people and help them to achieve something and watch how your thoughts on yourself will improve. We all need social support, and to be supportive to another means you are being supportive to yourself. Boosting someone else's confidence will boost your self-esteem in return.

Boosting another means you are willing to get in the trenches with them and help them out. Another definition of boost is to push or shove from below. That means you undergird them and give them a gentle shove in the right direction. We learned about "getting low" earlier in this chapter. Getting in a low place to help give someone a boost to a new level will keep you in good spirits and keep negativity away.

Boasting is not an attribute you want to have. Boasting is defined as a statement in which you express too much pride in yourself or in something you have, have done, or are connected to in some way. When you begin to brag on the things you have materialistically or the gifts God has given to you, it is equated to you stealing God's glory. Everything you possess should always glorify Him, not man. Do not exult yourself, because you are not God.

If you are constantly speaking in an excessive manner or always bringing the conversation back to you, you probably are boasting. Boasting is reflective of a pride issue. No one wants to be around, let alone be friends with, someone who only talks about them self all the time. Having things is nice, but having friends seems much more tangible. You can sit and count your money over and over, but you can never count on it to truly be there.

"And what do you benefit if you gain the whole world but lose your soul? Is there anything worth more than your soul" (Matthew 16:26, NLT)? Who wants material possessions so much that you do not gain everlasting life? You must really evaluate what is a priority in your life, and do some shifting in areas if you are

dealing with this negative character flaw. You will only get so far in life when you begin to boast. It will keep you separated and push people away.

People are attracted to people who can listen. When you boast, you are not able to listen. You turn a deaf ear because you are too caught up in yourself. You tune out the conversation of another just to be able to talk about yourself. That will keep people from becoming or staying as friends, because they can't talk to you.

If you want to build up your inner man, you first have to learn to boost yourself. Doing good things for others will help boost your self-esteem. Seeing others happy will bring happiness to your own soul. Believing in yourself will help you build your inner man. You have to first believe in yourself for you to begin to be able to accomplish the things you desire.

Keeping your spirit high is crucial for maintaining that happiness. You don't just want euphoria, but you want consistency. You have to find ways to stay positive. You have to try to focus on the pleasures of life; the simple things always bring happiness. Here are a couple things you can do to have a more consistent happiness and in turn boost your self-esteem.

Go for a walk out in nature. That will help uplift your spirit. There is nothing like being out in what God created. Studies have proven that people who were hospitalized recovered quicker with a view of nature than those who saw a brick wall. Just breathing fresh air and walking in a change of scenery will increase a good mood. Being outdoors, hearing the birds, seeing the length of the sky, feeling the sun on your skin, and smelling the aromas of life around you will cause a boost to your mood.

You can also listen to music. New research suggests that listening to music can lift your mood and ultimately lead to a greater quality of life. By simply listening to an upbeat song you can effectively boost your mood. Giving yourself a boost in happiness will build your inner man up and cause a shift in your overall life. You don't have to pursue happiness; you can actually attain it with a positive attitude and an optimistic mindset. If you learn how to boost yourself and others, boasting won't be an issue for you.

Beauty Tips

Cheeks are a simple thing that can really add life to your look. You can make your cheeks look higher, and your smile brighter by wearing a little make up. Adding some blush can add a sparkle to your face. It will apply color to your face and make you feel brighter, and lighter. These tips will help you in adding some luster to your look.

~For a youthful glow apply blush to the apples of your cheeks.

~Always smile when applying your blush to help bring out those "apples".

~To help your blush last throughout the day apply a sheer cream blush first, and then apply a powder blush. This gives a foundation and creates longevity.

A Simple Prayer

Here is a prayer to help you overcome pride and keep you from being boastful.

    Lord God, I just thank for who you are. I honor and glorify your name. God, I just want to say thank you for keeping me in your goodness. I pray that I never think higher of myself than I should, God. I pray, Lord, for humility at all times. Let my heart stay after your own, Jesus. I pray, God, that as I continue to lift you up, that you continue to draw all men unto you. Please let them see you in everything that I do. I pray Matthew 5:16 over myself. Let my light shine before them that they might see your good ways reflected and let them magnify your name. God, I pray that you help me let go of pride. I ask that you remove this plague from out of my life. I do not want to fail you, Lord, so I ask that you help me in the area of boasting and that you rid this false idol of self from out of my life. I give it to you, God, and I start fresh. I know that pride comes before the fall, so I thank you for giving me the warning before the destruction. I speak change to my attitude and I keep my eyes to the hills, for you, Lord, are my help. In you I find my boost, and in you is where I find my happiness. There is nothing in this world I desire more than you. There is no thing I have ever had that was greater than you. You, God, are the source of my strength and I love you with all my being.

In Jesus name, Amen.

Chapter 7

Self-Consciousness vs. Self-Awareness

To be self-conscious means that you are uncomfortably nervous about, or embarrassed by, what other people think about you. You become ill at ease by the perceptions others have of you. Why worry what someone's opinion is, if that opinion will not in any way assist you in becoming a better person? Why would you allow another's thoughts to cloud your own judgment on yourself? You have to be confident in you.

It is ok to be conscious of oneself but not self-conscious. There is quite a difference. To be conscious of oneself is to be conscious of one's own acts or states belonging to, or originating in, you. Therefore, you are intensely aware of you as an individual. That type of consciousness is absolutely acceptable.

To be conscious of you is to be self-aware. Self-awareness is defined as knowledge and awareness of your own personality or character. This is the moment you have an awakening of you. You have fallen in love and come into alignment with who God says that you are. You want to be assured in who you are.

FINDING ME IN THE MESS

Self-awareness is not just enough to know inside only your head. It is very important to showcase it. Self-awareness will cause you to be comfortable in your own skin. Your personality and character will be highlighted by your consciousness of who you think that you are. If your character is flawed, then you'd better believe that yourself awareness is flawed.

Let's look at consciousness and unconsciousness to use as an example. To be conscious is to be aware. To be aware you have to be awake. Therefore, you need to be roused in who you think that you are. Once you wake up, you will become alert and be able to begin a new journey.

We wake up each morning and begin a new day. The sun rises and we are to go out and start fresh. How can you begin again when you have no clue that it is a new day because you are asleep within yourself? How can you make your dreams come true when you have slept through each dawn? You will never bring your dreams to fruition if you never come out of your slumber.

You are constantly sleeping because you are completely unconscious. One definition of unconscious is: to be not awake especially due to injury, drug, etc. Are you so injured by low self-esteem that you have allowed yourself to become unconscious? Has the drug of "ignorance-is-bliss" become your life's motto and you continuously inject it into your veins, so you do not have to be aware that life could be so much more? It is time to arise and let go of the addiction of abuse to your consciousness.

If you go through life unconscious for a long period of time it can really affect you. You can cause your spirit to go into a coma-like state, where you walk through life in a daze. You will have no care as to what is going on in or around you. Being unconscious to self will cause you to have personality defects. As I mentioned above, it may cause character flaws.

Let's talk about some personality defects. Personality defects are things you do that cause unhappiness to yourself or others. Maybe you are easily irritated or are short tempered. You may find yourself being forgetful or lazy. There are many things that may be in your personality that shouldn't be. Once you become aware of whom you are, you will become more aware of these negative things and can begin to rid yourself of them.

It is the same with character flaws. Character and personality are alike, but different. Personality is the surface of a person and character is the depth of a person. It is easy to want to like what you already like, but you have to look into a person's heart. Personality can try to mask the deeper issues of someone. You must find their true colors.

Looking at your true character takes time, but in developing self-awareness it is a must. How can you fix what you do not know is broken? Take the time to look inside yourself and line yourself up with His word and see if God reveals some character flaws within you. I remember when I began my self-evaluation I had trust issues and I was quick to lie because of them. I didn't want to reveal all of me, and I hid behind the walls I put up. God showed me how this was hindering me from having friendships, love and life all together. I quickly began to change these things, so I could lead a happier and more productive life.

The Bible says *"And no one puts new wine into old wineskins. For the old skins would burst from the pressure, spilling the wine and ruining the skins. New wine is stored in new wineskins so that both are preserved"* (Matthew 9:17, NLT). Are you the new wine skins or the old? Do you have flexibility within you that God is able to use you? Can He pour His wine in you and not have to worry about it spilling out of all the holes that low self-esteem has created? Old wine skins are used and stretched out and He cannot produce inside of an unyielding vessel.

It is much better to be conscious of yourself than it is to be self-conscious of yourself. You have to be able to recognize who you are inside of God. If you come into the knowledge of you in Him then life will be much easier. When you are awakened by The Lord you will never want to fall asleep again because you will be awakened to the desires He has for you. You will begin to pursue eternal life not just life here on earth, but something much deeper.

Once you get through tilling your garden, allow people to plant great seed and allow others the opportunity to water your ground, then God can bring forth the increase. Gardens take time to look beautiful and nourished because it is a process. As you grow you will have to pull the weeds that will try to choke out your growth. The weeds would be all those character flaws, and as you begin to uproot the bad you will see those great seeds begin to sprout and eventually you will begin to flourish. You will grow and blossom into a beautiful garden that God can easily maintain.

Also, give yourself enough space to grow. We all grow at different rates but you have to have room to grow. Do not try to develop like someone else because God called you to be unique and peculiar. You may see a rose, and say, "I am definitely a rose" because you like the care and tutelage they receive. Yet, you may not even realize that you are an easier type of flower that is able to stand on its own without so much maintenance. If you are a gardenia become confident in your ability to bloom with ease. Thank God for creating you that way.

If you are the rose, you as well must learn to love yourself. Do not worry about the thorns you have because, like Paul, they are there to remind you to not become conceited. Your beauty is something of great revelation and spoke of quite frequently, but those thorns will keep you humble. Embrace them and know that God's strength is made perfect in your weakness. Find the depth in you beyond just the beauty of your makeup. For that you must venture beyond just wearing makeup and begin to understand the depths of God inside of you.

Yes, be self-aware but beware not to become big headed. There is a thin line between confidence and conceit. Hold your head high and walk with a sense of pride, but do not turn your nose up and walk proud. Balance yourself by filling yourself with God's word. As I told you earlier in this book, lean on Him not to your own understanding. Above all, allow Him to direct your path.

Allow the Son to shine on you and then bloom in the light of His glory. Trust Holy Spirit to rain down on you and fill you with living water. Rely on God to feed you His good word, and like with manna you will be refueled each day. These are the things needed for your garden to grow and flourish. These are the three key ingredients for your roots to take root and for you to spring up and grow.

No garden is unmanageable; it just needs some TLC. Only Jesus can give you the time and love you desire. Only God can plant inside you what needs to grow. Allow Him to turn your soil over and get you ready to produce. He sees the potential, so give Him the keys to your secret garden and He will open up the gates of the beauty of you.

My story continued...

As I told you, my home life played a huge role in my behavior. My father was very sick and had just had a stroke. He was no longer able to do certain things and needed a lot of assistance. My mother, unable to give him around the clock care, placed him in a nursing home. It was a hard adjustment for me.

I was used to my dad being outside, sitting on the porch, waiting for me to walk up from my bus. We hung out sometimes and watched MacGyver and Matlock, but sickness took that all away. I was frustrated by this fact and was unable to handle those feelings, so I lashed out. There was no guarantee that he would come back from this, and that was a hard pill for me to swallow. My actions displayed my turmoil greatly, but no one noticed until it was too late.

By this point I was already dressing and acting differently. I was a 15-year-old on paper, but a grown adult in my mind. If my mom would have been in the right mental state to check me, it would have been a passing phase. My mother was dealing with so much at that time though that worrying about her young teenage daughter was not of the upmost importance. That was not the best plan, nor one she intentionally intended to have, but for her it was the easiest. My life spun out of control, and I found myself dizzy from the commotion but instead of getting off the dance floor I let myself continue to twirl and spin.

Then my dad had a second stroke and this one took away his speech. This was devastating because now he could think but couldn't tell us what was on his mind. His voice was trapped inside him. Words formed without a way to be released. This sank him into depression.

My heart hurt for him and I think we all knew the inevitable was around the corner. On the morning of March11, 2000, we got the news we all so dreaded to get. My amazing father had passed away. I was heartbroken and nothing at that time was able to balm that wound. I no longer cared at all about anything because I was truly grief stricken.

I allowed the waves of emotions to carry me. I set sail on an ocean of feelings and based everything off my heart. That is the worst thing you could ever do. Never make decisions based off of emotions or you will lose you. Your decisions have to be directed by stability, and the only thing that never changes is God.

After Daddy died, I felt like a lot of me died with him. The truth of the matter is; I did allow myself to die. Dead things can't grow and I didn't. I chose to sleep walk through life. I was knocked unconscious, but it was by my choosing that I stayed in that coma-like state.

After my dad passed away I went from just being a window display to actively participating in my self-destruction. I desired love from a male and I unintentionally wanted it any way I could get it. If a guy showed interest in me I gave him attention back. This was the beginning of my worth totaling out to zero. I was in a downward spiral, and I couldn't get out of the whirlwind.

I knew the road I was walking was going to lead to destruction, but I wanted to blaze that trail. I had no self-worth and not one care for better. I was hurting so bad and it seemed no one knew it but me. No one noticed my hand reaching out of despair, searching for help. If they did, they didn't care, so I, too, didn't care.

To be continued...

(Healing)

Dress for Success

"Strength and honour are her clothing; and she shall rejoice in time to come" **(Proverbs 31:25).**

Have you had times where you have felt weak, where you have felt undesirable? Yes, we all have, but this scripture is so powerful to me because it gives us confirmation that we can clothe ourselves in strength and honor. It tells us of the great that is due to come. When we are weak, God is our strength, when we feel like nothing, God then becomes everything. We will rejoice in due season.

What are you dressing yourself in? When you feel less, then you dress cheaply. When you feel lonely or mad, happy or sad, your outward appearance will always reflect your inner feelings. You truly will be dressing the part. When your mind shifts, so will your appearance.

In the above scripture it is a mother telling her son the type of woman he should marry. This is the Proverbs 31 woman. She is the role model of all role models for women. The beauty of her is the truth women search for. She surely is the prototype.

In this scripture it says that strength and honor are her clothing. Therefore, she awakes every morning and brushes away the trials of yesterday and strengthens herself in prayer and the things of today. Why allow the cares of the world to carry you into stress and confusion? It is much easier to just focus on the things you can change. Strengthen yourself in what you are able to do.

Place honor on yourself and wear that garment with boldness. You have no reason to feel unloved and unwanted, because God so loves you. His word says *"For God so loved the world, that he gave his only begotten Son, that whosoever believeth in him should not perish, but have everlasting life"* (John 3:16). God places honor on you and has destined you for greatness. He sent his only Son to die for you because He loves and honors you that much.

Honor should be a part of your daily dress because where there is favor there is honor. God honors what He favors and you, my dear, give favor. Yes, the Bible says that when a man finds a wife, he finds a good thing and obtains favor from The Lord. A man gets favor when he finds his wife. Yes, woman, you bring favor to your husband.

The bible says *"For the Lord God is a sun and shield; the Lord bestows favor and honor; no good thing does he withhold from those who walk is blameless" (*Psalm 84:11, NIV). Favor and honor go hand in hand. When you honor God, He favors you. When you walk uprightly he places favor on you. Do not allow low self-esteem to destroy your high moral standards and keep you from walking upright and into the favor of God.

Dressing in strength and honor is exactly what you should do each day. Wrap those garments around you like scarves to keep the cold bite of low self-esteem from nipping at you. Learn from this scripture and let it reflect in your mind, so you can begin to allow these things to be worn on your heart. As you adorn yourself with the essence of strength and honor you will begin to adore yourself. When you adore yourself, others will begin to adore you as well.

As time passes by, you will be able to rejoice. As happiness enters your life and sadness departs, you will feel a joy inside that causes you to rejoice. As you stand in God and live by His word you will be able to laugh at the future. You do not have to worry or fear over anything because you put your trust in The Lord. Stand tall in Christ, and know that you are equipped, and as you prepare to be prepared, smile, for your future looks bright.

In life it is important to dress for success. You have to look like where you want to go. If you look in corporate America, you will see the business casual look. Most of the people I know that work in the field of corporate America do not have to speak to customers in person but only over the phone. Yet, you still have to dress like you're the CEO of your job. Walk in there boldly and expect His light to shine.

You have to dress for the part. Actors have to dress like the character they're playing. They have to live up to the persona they're portraying. If they are acting as a business man, then they have to dress in suits because that is how they dress. If you want a job in that type of industry you don't want to come to the interview as a woman in a tight miniskirt or as a man in jeans and tennis shoes.

FINDING ME IN THE MESS

Though you may dress that way in your day to day life, it would not be wise to show up in anything besides business attire.

Why is it important to look the part? It is crucial that you look like you're headed in the right direction. If you look confident, confidence then begins to look for you. If you dress for where you are heading, the future will present itself to you. Greatness shouldn't just be in you; it should be on you too.

As you begin to change the way you dress, you begin to grow inside who you are. You will learn your likes and dislikes. You will develop your sense of style. Dressing for success gives you access into what your future holds. You have opportunities become available to you when you look the part.

Dressing nice doesn't just help you move up in your job, or give you more opportunities. What it does, though, is help in making you feel better. When you dress nicely, it makes you feel good. Dressing nicely gives you confidence all by itself. When you feel good, you start to become a better person.

The question now is, what feels right? Well, you have to take the time to find your flavor. You have to understand what fits your body and flatters your shape. Begin to try things out and step out of the box while doing it. Try new things on, be free and have fun.

Look up information online about your body type. Learn all you can and see what others with the same shape wear. If you like it, go ahead and find the outfit, or something similar, and try it on. If you like it, buy it. Then rock that and watch your confidence soar.

One thing I do want to say is: give you the time of pampering yourself. It is ok to sometimes buy yourself something nice. As a hard working woman, a mother, a wife or a teenager, you deserve a little gift to yourself every now and again. You can shop at thrift stores, consignment shops, whatever you want. Give yourself a quarterly allowance or however you choose to do it and go buy something nice. Take a day at the spa, go to the movies or drive to another state and site see. Whatever is just do it and enjoy that time for you.

I would also say get the opinion of your closest girl friend, sister or from your hubby or kids. It helps to have another opinion besides your own. Sometimes our friends see what we missed. Your husband would be good because he knows what he likes on you. The reason I say your children is because they are just brutally honest and will always tell you the truth whether you want to hear it or not.

Another thing I did was find my color. There is always that one color that looks great on you. I love bright colors; they make me happy. The best colors on me are yellow and orange. Find your color and rock it.

When you find the color, you will then find the clothes, and you will then ultimately feel good, then the sky won't even be the limit for you. When you are able to dress for success, you will begin to believe that success is attainable. Dressing for where you want to go can only help in getting you to that very destination. Take the time to give yourself the bold statement of confidence just by your dress. It really is a simple way to give you a boost in self-esteem.

Take the time to find what fits right and you will have all the time to feel right. Feeling right is half the battle, and it will help free up insecurities and bad moods. Success is defined as the correct or desired result of an attempt. Therefore, if you attempt to make each day count, eventually they will. If you wake up, get up and get dressed with success in mind, then you will have access to the keys that unlock all the doors of success. The door is there waiting to be unlocked and opened, go ahead and knock on the door of success. Access is granted!

Beauty Tips

Dressing right is important for where you are going, or trying to go, in life. It is critical to have the right dress, the right perfume, and the right looks overall. You want to be comfortable and confident all at the same time. How you look really will help in determining who will look at you, for a promotion, the initial job, etc. Here are a few tips for this particular area.

~A good perfume will consist of a balanced mix of notes that blend well with your natural smell. Try a bit out before you buy anything, and make sure you like how it smells on you.

~Accessorize in bright colors. If you like neutrals, add energy with boldly hued accessories.

~Embrace your shape. Know what you look right in and don't sway because something is a new style or trend. Find what flatters your silhouette and stick with it.

A Simple Prayer

Here is a prayer to help you fight against self-consciousness and help you to be successful.

     Lord God, I thank you for who you are and for bringing me into the fullness of who I am in you. I ask that you continue to help me know that I am fearfully and wonderfully made. I'm a marvelous work of yours, Lord, and I thank you for calling me to walk in that confidence. Jesus, I ask that you continue to help me become successful. Allow me to walk with assured steps into my future. Your word says to come boldly before the throne. Therefore, I ask that as I learn that boldness that I continue to carry it in every area of my life. Let me become bold in my speech and in my thoughts toward myself. Give me the boldness of you, Christ Jesus, and let me never waiver. I speak streams of success to flow into my life. I decree and declare that success is my portion and that wealth is attainable to me. I thank you that I will dress for success and gain access to the many doors of success. I thank you that I will find exactly what fits me and flatters me and that it will be comfortable for me. I thank you that as I change my outward appearance that my inward appearance be molded and corrected as well. I am yours and I pray to always have favor in your sight, Lord. Thank you for loving me and helping me become better.

In Jesus name, Amen.

Chapter 8

Hiding Yourself Inside of Being Timid

Are you timid? First, let me define what timid means. Timid is defined as feeling or showing a lack of courage or confidence. Have you ever been in a situation where you needed to be brave but you just couldn't muster up the guts to do it? We all have, I am sure, but it's when those times become an everyday function in your life that there is a problem.

When I think of timid, I think of the cowardly lion in the Wizard of Oz. He was so afraid in his mind that it held him back from being who God had created him to be. Lions are fearless; they are the kings of the jungle. He should have seen himself as the king, the top of the food chain. Yet, in his mind, he was as terrified of life as cats are terrified of getting wet.

His mind hadn't caught up to the revelation of self just yet. His mind was conditioned by his behavior. If you act frightened, you will become fearful. The word clearly states *"The Lord is my light and my salvation; whom shall I fear? The Lord is the strength of my life; of whom shall I be afraid?* (Psalm 27:1). You do not have to be scared. Remember God didn't give you the spirit of fear.

What God gave us is much more. The Bible states *"For God hath not given us the spirit of fear; but of power, and of love, and of a sound mind"* (2 Timothy 1:7). Those are some of the strongest tools that He gave you to battle with. When you step out on faith to win the war you better know how to tread those rough and high waters. If not, you may find yourself in over your head.

Is there no boldness inside of you? Is there no determination or drive within you? Boldness causes you to be determined. It causes you to see the job through to the end. When you have boldness a drive resonates inside you, propelling you into action.

Esther was driven by boldness. She went before the King's throne unsummoned to save her people. Her determination was caused by boldness. That audaciousness she had was given to her by God. Ask The Lord to give you a bold nature, so you can develop stronger in determination and gain more drive.

The Bible tells us *"Let us therefore come boldly unto the throne of grace that we may obtain mercy, and find grace to help in time of need"* (Hebrews 4:16). You must go in confidence to God to receive mercy and grace in your time of struggle. If you need God to extend grace to you, you can't go and ask shyly and fearfully. You know you need it, and when you need something you have to be bold enough to ask for that help. Approach God like you mean it, show Him that you need Him and He will give you the thing that you are seeking.

By the time it was over Esther had not only gone before the King unsummoned, which was a death sentence to do that. She did it with a bold spirit and because of that she was received with his scepter being held out to her. When you have boldness, nothing that is for you can be withheld from you. When God gives you boldness, He gives you His approval, and you will break the mold of rules that are set and be given divine favor. Just like Esther broke the rules put in place because God was involved in her being valiant.

Being timid is being shy. We all have been shy before, that is common, but when your shyness becomes crippling and gives you social anxiety, that is going beyond the norm. Having that type of shyness is when it is not just a moment of experiencing something new but a spirit that has attached itself to you. It is ok, when first introduced to a new thing, to be a little timid or nervous because you have never done it before. Maybe when you first meet someone you shy away. Yes, that is normal. When you totally avoid anything new, when you can't handle change and you become overly fearful and resistant to anything that is new; that is a spirit.

The Bible says that God has not given us the spirit of fear. If God didn't give us the spirit of fear, why would you allow it to reside inside you? Fear has no place inside your heart, so evict that spirit immediately. Do not allow fear to take up residence within your being. Rebuke that spirit and cast it far away from your thoughts, so you will not be influenced by it.

How do you get rid of fear? The Bible says *"There is no fear in love; but perfect love casteth out fear: because fear hath torment. He that feareth is not made perfect in love"* (1 John 4:18). What does this mean? What is perfect love?

Perfect love consists around a true experience in God. Perfect is defined as whole or complete. Therefore, you need a whole love, not a partial form of love, but something that is solid or concrete. This type of love can only be found inside a relationship with God. When Christ died on the cross, he said "it is finished." That translates to it is done, it is complete. That display on Calvary was the epitome of perfect love, so Christ is perfect love.

We search all of our lives for that "perfect love," our soul mate. The only person who can complete you is Christ because He gave you life. A spouse can add to you, but not complete you; they can love you, but not love you perfectly. They will mess up sometimes, but God has perfected love and it is in covenant with Him that you become perfected by love. It is in His love, true relationship to Christ, that fears will be expelled by His perfect love.

Why not find what you are longing for in Jesus? For the word stated above says that fear is torment. Why would you allow yourself to be punished by fear? Remember, God gave you love, power and a sound mind; so you have love to push out fear, you have the power to bind it up and cast it away and you have the stability in your mind to not allow it to represent you. Be perfected in God's love and get rid of the fear that being timid produced.

Let's talk about how being overly shy is a disadvantage to you. If you are extremely shy you run the risk of not capitalizing on the moments that God ordains for you. You may never get the position you are qualified for or desire because shyness will keep you from going for it. Friendships may not be easy to have or hold on to because being timid keeps you from starting conversations. Being timid is a disservice to you and to your dreams.

Shyness can cause the fear of rejection. When rejection sets in as a coupled spirit to timidity you will begin to reject yourself to keep from being rejected. Does that make sense? Fear of rejection causes you to reject you because it will make you believe you are not able to attain what you are hoping to have. Therefore, to make it easier you simply take yourself out of the equation of that dream, even though you have no clue if you would have had the chance to have what you wanted.

Rejecting yourself is manifest as the spirit of self-sabotage. You fail because you never tried to succeed. The Bible says to have a friend one must show themselves friendly. Timid people tend to have a harder time showing friendliness, not because they are arrogant, but because they are standoffish. Quietness isn't a conversation starter and bashfulness is not an ice breaker.

Psychologytoday.com says not only does excessive shyness lead to greater loneliness and poorer quality relationships, it can also lead to problems with emotional well-being such as depression. It is crucial that you develop confidence in yourself because without it your life will be greatly impacted by the negative. Stop hiding inside of shyness. Go ahead and take life by the horns and walk it out boldly.

My Story Continued...

My self-sabotage began pretty much right after my father passed away. I found myself doing things I would never do, dating guys I would never date and just being overtly outrageous in my behavior. It was easier for me to be desired than to be alone. Alone was a very bad place for me at that time. I wasn't suicidal, but I was a ticking time bomb and idleness could have been my fuse.

FINDING ME IN THE MESS

I stayed busy but it was the wrong type of busyness. I started hanging around people that meant me no good. They were alike to who I was at that time, but not the real me. They were girls who were fast and I became that too. I hung around guys that would sleep with me but not stay with me.

Truly I had commitment issues and trust issues. There was no desire in me to want to be loved but it was a false pretense because my heart's desire was to love and be loved. I made myself believe it was easier to have a brief no-strings-attached relationship to these men. Just lay it on them strong and get out of there before they try to make me their forever-and-a-day. It was entirely the wrong mentality to have.

As time went on I slept around and gave away my goods, never realizing that soon there would be nothing left to give because I would be used up goods. I had no clue or care of the damage I was doing to me. The emotional emptiness I felt was like an echo in the wilderness. No one heard the cries from the barren land inside of me.

I cried with no feeling, I fought with no fight, and I was drowning with no life guard near. I gave me away piece by piece and with each piece I gave I went more and more under the waters of self-destruction. I gave the impression that life was good. I gave the appearance of happiness, but I was so miserable that it shocks me to look back on it. The innocent little bright eyed girl was gone and in her place stood this strange, awkward, phony, wide eyed promiscuous teenager. I longed for help, but had no idea where to find it or even where to start.

Guys treated me how I presented myself. I was easy and they all knew it. Do not think for a second that you can sleep around and everybody not know about it because it becomes everyone's business and rumors will swarm you like bees around their honey. I told myself I didn't care, but deep down I did, I was just trying to save face. Yet, I gave access to my personal bank account and time after time I found my self-worth depleted and my funds overdrawn.

I had to keep them from making deposits with counterfeit money. I had to put an out-of-order sign on me and try to work on myself. I was in operation save me. How was I going to fix something so broken? How was I going to renovate something so dilapidated? There was the initial problem…I was trying to fix me.

I cut off those I was around and my mom changed our surroundings but all that did was cause those issues to lie dormant inside of me. Dormant isn't delivered, remember that. Dormant is just a brief hiatus to issues that are still living inside of you. It is just a problem unsolved. There, but just glanced at and quickly breezed over, but nevertheless there. I had a problem that I needed solved but I thought sweeping it under the rug was the correct answer. Oh, how wrong I was.

To be continued...

(Healing)

Eyes Highlight I

"The light of the body is the eye: if therefore thine eye be single, thy whole body should be full of light" **(Matthew 6:22).**

This scripture is talking about the inner man being the light of the body. Our inner man is what gives light so that we can see. In the Bible it says *"The spirit of the man is the candle of the Lord, searching all inward parts of the belly"* (Proverbs 20:27). Therefore, it reflects the light of God in us and shines outwardly to help us find our way. Understand it like this: it is like a light house guiding ships out on the ocean to safety. God's light shines in us and reflects out to bring us safely through the storms on the ocean of life.

So, the light of the body is our inner man. If, therefore, thine eye be single, if your inner man is clean without any build up or residue, you should be seeing clearly because you are in proper working order. That is why we first must clean ourselves out, so that we may be in working order to guide the rest of the body into God's marvelous light. We cannot have spiritual cataracts and hope to help someone have proper vision. It is time we get those cataracts removed and have God insert a lens that will gather no build up or cloudiness and help us to see with better clarity.

The Bible says *"You hypocrite, first take the plank out of your own eye, and then you will see clearly to remove the speck from your brother's eye"* (Matthew 7:5, NIV). In order to make your inner man single you must remove the sleep and crust out of it and take time to begin to gain focus. You have to wake up and pray, seek God and allow Him to shine the light on your path. Allow Him to shine His light on the dark places that are hidden from your vision. Then you can begin to correct those hidden things and produce a light that will showcase a good and bright ray and draw people to magnify your Father in heaven.

Did you know that your eyes truly are the windows to your soul? There are so many things you can find out about a person just by looking into their eyes. For many years I worked as an Optician and then as an Ophthalmic Technician. These are two very different jobs but both deal with the eyes. Eyes truly tell a story.

As an optician I worked to help people see correctly. If they had an issue seeing far away or close up I worked to correct their vision. We would prescribe corrective lenses to help them see well. They would pick out the glasses and we would put the proper lens in to help them have the best visual acuity possible. I dealt with measurements and appearance and it was fun, but did you know there is a huge difference between seeing and vision?

When I began working in the field of Ophthalmology I understood what vision really is all about. In this line of work, you do not so much focus on only how well they see, but even more on the health of their vision. We looked at the health of the eye and the quality of life given from their vision. We had to make very tough and heartbreaking decisions for the patients in our care. It was as rewarding as it was heart breaking.

That is one of the focuses in this healing part of the chapter, having vision vs. just seeing. Also, we will discuss how to clean you out and what eyes highlight I mean. I want you to begin to get your quality of life back. I hope to show you how to no longer try to focus so much on the quantity of your life, but the quality of your life. Life truly is what you choose to make it.

Seeing is defined as having the ability to see: to have the power of sight. Your eyes were created to give you sight. They are there so you know where you are physically going. They enable you to perform better because you can see what you are doing. Your eyes help you to perceive the things around you. Seeing is examining, discovering and recognizing things to get a better understanding of them.

Vision is defined as the act of seeing. Vision is the action of seeing. You can see but can still have no vision. Vision is a step beyond just simply seeing. We can look at something and perceive it how we choose to, but when you use vision you conceive what is really there. Does that make sense?

You want to get in touch with vision. Allow your inner man to work with the Holy Spirit. That is what we are missing. We have to allow our light to be orchestrated by Holy Spirit. When you go to the movies there is someone up there controlling the projector on the screen. Allow Holy Spirit to control your light and you will see beyond seeing.

When you learn to give control to Holy Spirit then your natural eye and spiritual eye will work in sync with one another. You will have spiritual binocularity. That is both eyes working together as if one. Killing your flesh will produce more spirit. You must remember that you are spirit first, not the other way around. Gain vision not just visual acuity. Seeing is fine but having vision is much better and will upgrade your spiritual understanding and discernment.

What does eyes highlight eye mean? This means that your eyes highlight you both naturally and spiritually. As I stated above, when testing someone's eyes you can see what is going on within them. You can see diseases like diabetes, high cholesterol, STD's, etc. All of these different things can be found just by studying the eyes.

Even on a surface level you can look into a person's eyes and see what they are dealing with. Craziness is often displayed in the eyes of a person suffering from that spirit. You can usually see deception in the eyes. You can surely see rage and anger. You can see sadness or sleep deprivation. All of these things, and more, can be easily seen just by looking into their eyes.

You want a good highlight from your eyes. You want your eyes to reveal happiness, joy, optimism, wisdom, understanding, kindness, etc. Your eyes should showcase the stability of who you are in Christ. They should reflect your likeness to Christ. Your outward eyes and inner man (eyes) should have a light that reflects out and can shine for someone who is lost in darkness, and should not cast a shadow of more darkness.

You can begin to have a better highlight of you by cleaning yourself up. You can have more hope by having your mind stayed in Christ. Then your thoughts would be linked into His thoughts and as we all should know *"For I know the thoughts that I think toward you, saith the Lord, thoughts of peace, and not of evil, to give you an expected end* (Jeremiah 29:11). God wants to give us an expected in.

Once you walk in that confidence, life will be much more pleasant. You won't focus on what this life has to offer you but what you can offer the people in your life. They say you only live once, but that is far from the truth. There is a better way of living and that is living in Christ. When you clean yourself out, you will be allowing God to do a complete cornea transplant and your eyes really will highlight you. The cornea is the eye's outermost layer and it must remain transparent to refract light properly. Living totally in Jesus gives you properly refracted light.

    Allowing God to begin to clean you up and clean you out is the best way to get the maximum usage out of your light. Your shine does better when the dust and debris are cleared away. When you remove what is covering your brightness, then people will see your light clearly. *"Neither do men light a candle, and put it under a bushel, but on a candlestick; and it gives light unto all that are in the house"* (Matthew 5:15). Your light should easily shine and should create a glow for everyone to be able to see.

    God can easily clean you up because He loves to do the cleaning. We are not able to fix ourselves quite the way He can. The problem most of us have is that we say "let me get myself together and then I will come to God." No, God says "come as you are" and He will fix the areas that need to be fixed and they will actually stay corrected. When we try to fix ourselves we just put a bandage over the area, but God applies pressure to stop the bleeding, then cleans out all the dirt inside the wound, stitches up the deep cuts and applies Neosporin to the surface level abrasions. God truly is the Great Physician.

    The Lord longs to take us from where we are to where we need to be. His desire is to see us made whole. He wants us totally dependent on Him. Don't you know that you no longer have to bleed out because Jesus already bled and died for you? You only need to let Him mend you and then just simply rest in Him. You are the light of the world, so shine bright and let your rays of his Sonshine break through the darkness.

Beauty Tips

Your eyes are probably one of your best features on your face. Eyes capture beauty and should reflect that same beauty. Take the time to highlight your eyes. Let them show the inner beauty of you. These beauty tips will help you do just that.

~Darker colors recede, lighter colors bring out.

~When wearing lashes; be sure to measure them first, and if you need to trim them, cut from the outer corner, never the inner corner.

~Don't forget mascara for your bottom lashes.

A Simple Prayer

Here is a prayer to help push you out into being courageous in and through God.

     Hello Father, I love you and thank you for being God in my life. I want to say thank you for being who you are. I want to acknowledge your goodness and faithfulness. I ask you to continue to help me improve in my self-esteem. I ask that the shy part of me be brought to the forefront and my boldness be drawn out. I declare that I will not be timid but that I will be a bright light shining forth. I thank you for causing my light to break the darkness of the world around me. Allow my light in you, oh God, to shine so bright that it leads people out of bondage. I speak to my confidence and say speak up and speak out. Let my voice echo in you Lord Jesus, let them hear you in everything I speak. I decree that I will be a city on a hill that can't be hidden. I will shine my light for the entire world to see. I will not shy away, I will not hide, but I will stand out and reflect your light. Thank you for increasing inside me. Thank you for showering me in perfect love, and through your perfect love casting out all fear inside of me. I am whole and complete inside of you, Christ Jesus, and I will forever stand in boldness. I will forever remain yours.

In Jesus name, Amen.

Chapter 9

Beating Promiscuity

This chapter is about the strong man that held me captive. This was the thing I struggled with most during the years of low self-esteem. I was very promiscuous. I had no regard for myself. I allowed myself to be used and manipulated.

Let's talk about promiscuity. What exactly does that word mean? Promiscuous is defined as having or involving many sexual partners. So, promiscuity is promiscuous sexual behavior. There is no limit to one particular person and you act out in total carelessness.

Low self-esteem causes this spirit to attach itself to people sometimes. In my case, it did. You would not think a person dealing with low self-esteem would have the confidence to have multiple sex partners, let alone one. Au contraire my loves, self-confidence is not how you act, but how you think first and then outwardly display it. It definitely can manifest in this nature.

Usually if you are dealing with promiscuity it could be linked to low self-esteem. You would more than likely use sex as a way to be noticed. You are attention seeking because you want to feel good about yourself. Yet you may not even realize that this will only bring negative attention. If you do not know that you are in such a detrimental state, you will not care that you are acting so wildly for the time frame that it persists.

For that moment, you receive a self-satisfying high off of this risky behavior. You feel fulfilled and wildly free but really all you are doing is clanking more and more chains of bondage around yourself. When you are continuously appeasing your flesh and having a flesh fest, you eventually become a slave to lust. Then you get stuck in this emotional drainage rut. You then have to continue to do what has become familiar to you. Sadly, you remain caught up with this familiar lust spirit.

Lust is a spirit that cares nothing about how or who. It simply must have. That demon wants to be satisfied and unfortunately it never can be satisfied. It is like a black hole, just sucking up everything that comes near it. Your desires become outrageous and sexual exploits are likened to a bottomless pit; there truly will be no end.

This is a spirit that is hard to break. It honestly will overtake every area of your life. You will become obsessed with sexual thoughts and sexual activity. Everything will be centered on sex. This spirit wrecks your life.

If self-esteem isn't properly cultivated at a young age, you can guarantee that the promiscuous behavior will continue on into adulthood. Young girls, especially need to be taught a sense of self-worth. You have to be taught that you are more than just a fling or a one-night stand. It is highly possibly detrimental in my mind to NOT be taught that you are precious treasure and to keep your goods buried until the right man comes along. It is best to be taught that your virginity is sacred and should only be given away once married. Learning to not give yourself away to who you thinks is the "right man", will keep you from giving your virginity to who you deem worthy because feelings like I said can cloud judgment. I understand this now but it took way too long for me to get the gist of it.

My dad died when I was 16. That was such a crucial time in my life. I was a young lady, no longer a child, but still not a woman. I was in my second year of high school and so needed my father. He was who I looked to for my example of what a man should be. Losing him at such a critical age distorted my view and confused my understanding and I got lost somewhere in translation.

I suffered the loss of my virginity in such a devastating manner, three months later lost my dad, and about three months after that I was raped. I won't talk too much about the rape because that is an entirely different book all by itself. I want you to understand how and why promiscuity can attach itself to you. Lust is lust and it has no gender, no pretenses, it just simply is. It will take you down quickly though.

I was in a horrible place. I had just endured three major life experiences and all of them tragic on their own, but so close together as to be absolutely devastating. Life was anything but normal and stability had long since left. You search for change because your inner man knows that what you're doing isn't right but your flesh has been feeding off you like a leech and you are usually torn between two opinions.

The Bible says *"A double minded man is unstable in all his ways"* (James 1:8). Agreeing with your flesh and not subduing it causes you to become undecided in your mind. You then will come into agreement with something because it feels good to your flesh, but your spirit will know that it's wrong. When you are double-minded you become that way in every area of your life. Double-mindedness can easily and quickly lead to schizophrenia.

Being promiscuous is asking for a death sentence on a silver platter. It lies before you in your mind; a feast fit for kings, but it is filled with empty calories and processed sugars that give you a false sense of fulfillment and then leave you ravenous only an hour later. This type of food is unhealthy and can eventually lead to health problems and or death. You cannot eat fast food and sweets all the time and think that it is a healthy way of living. That lifestyle will eventually catch up to you.

Promiscuity is something that leaks into all parts of your life. It messes with you mentally and emotionally and affects you physically and spiritually. It is a like a leaking pipe that drips quietly and slowly at first, but over time that small sound becomes deafening and the slow drops create a huge mess. There is no amount of buckets that will catch the leak of that type of pipe. It is a pipe that is soon to burst due to all the damage.

Let me go into some of the ways it ruins your life. Obviously physically it can cause disease. You can catch STDs, some treatable and some not. Some are worse than others. The bad ones can cause you to become sterile. Like for example, Chlamydia and Gonorrhea can cause pelvic inflammatory disease and can cause infertility.

Of course there is HIV and AIDS. These two diseases are by far the worst amongst them all, in my opinion, because they eventually will kill you. Not only will your life be forever altered because they attack the body, it is a death sentence waiting to happen. You will live each day knowing that it is silently killing you. You are basically in prison, sitting on death row, knowing you are going to die but just not sure of when. Who wants to live like that?

You will also get spiritual issues. You are now dealing with all sorts of spirits from soul ties. You literally become a cesspool filled up with nasty spirits. As they sit around lounging inside you, you become further and further away from God. We all know a life without God is no life at all.

Mentally it warps your mind into believing that you deserve this treatment. The spirits whisper in your ear and say this is who you are. They brand your mind with derogatory thinking and clutter your thoughts with rejection. Mentally you cannot maintain and are constantly on edge. Your mind has no strength to cast down imaginations, so you live in some fantasy world parallel to reality.

Emotionally you become undone. You will become unglued, so to speak. You enter a time zone of constant emotional turmoil and your feelings become unturned. Your highs and lows mix together because you become numb to your feelings. Emotionally you become completely drained.

Promiscuity gives the illusion that it is a superstar lifestyle, but in reality it won't leave you rich or famous. It will send you to an early grave or hand you a less lustrous life. God came to give you an abundant life. Don't let satan counter offer God's offer with a far less amount than what you are worth. The enemy gives false hopes and fruitless dreams. What he offers will lead you down a path of destruction and will leave you empty, broken and alone.

More of My Story...

Now, that I was older I thought I was past everything. I had moved on from the situation and the people I once hung around. What I didn't realize is that you attract what you are. I removed myself from the situation, but I hadn't resolved the problem. Nothing good was coming my way because nothing good had been restored inside of me.

See, when dealing with issues of such magnitude you need deliverance. You can't be made free from something you have no clue that you are bound in. You also surely can't be made free when you do not know the Son. The Bible says *"If the Son therefore shall make you free, you shall be free indeed"* (John 8:36). When you allow Jesus residence inside you, He will then set you, as the captive, free and when He frees you, you are truly free.

I entered into another relationship and it was the same, but I thought it was different. He was older and had a good job and seemed so into me. I thought I had stumbled onto something great. I stumbled all right but what we had was not great. I had stumbled on my own foolish ignorance; and I saw what I wanted to see.

I watched him with other kids and said, "I know he would be a good father to a child if we had one." I then began to yearn for a daughter. My reasoning was horrible. I wanted her to love me and to need me. I wanted her to give me confidence in love and life again.

He and I never really discussed having a child, but we weren't doing anything to prevent a baby, so I tried and I got pregnant. I was 23 years old at the time, with a man I thought loved me, not married to him but pregnant with his child. My daughter was born and secrets were revealed. The man I thought I possibly had a future with had been lying to me the entire time. It was a mess beyond comprehension but let me just say I let go of the hope of him and me.

As time went on, life was not easy. I was a single mother in a cycle of addiction. I wanted better for my daughter but abuse doesn't care about any of that as long as it claims a victim. I was the fly caught in the spider's web and it was spinning me deeper into its web of destruction. I knew without help I eventually would be devoured by this thing I was in.

I still slept around but it was few and far between, or so I believed. The thing is, anyone outside of your husband is one too many. Also, my daughter didn't deserve that and surely didn't need to be around it. I never brought anyone around her and the couple of guys I dated after she was born were only allowed over if she was in bed. That is still not a good thing because what you allow in your atmosphere has right to claim the place it was given access to.

I never got too serious with anyone love-wise but I would still give them me physically, which is quite serious. I finally gave my heart to someone and once again it ended in heartbreak. By this point I was actually finally fed up. I couldn't take anymore and when I looked at my precious baby girl, I knew I had to give her better. Refusing to allow her life to be a product of my environment, I began to take small steps to change. My first step and best step was towards God; I knew only He could clean up the mess that was me. Only Christ could do this type of work that needed to be done and I sought him with all of my being.

To be continued...

(Healing)

Uncovered to Covered

"When I passed by you again and looked upon you, indeed your time was the time of love; so I spread My wing over you and covered your nakedness. Yes, I swore an oath to you and entered into a covenant with you, and you became Mine" says the Lord God" **(Ezekiel 16:8, NKJV).**

    This text is literally talking about God's entering into covenant with the people in the wilderness at Mt. Sinai but I want to draw from this text in its figurative form. God loves to love us. Yes, He delights in loving us and He wants to be in covenant with us. His desire is to cover our filthiness and clean us out. After He washes your sins away, you will be a beautiful bride.

    Sometimes it takes a second time for us to look and see the big picture. Something can be right in front of our eyes but we won't see it. We tend to see what we want to see, not always what is truly there. Once we take a second look we see the truth. You are more than what you think you are.

    You can be a wife. God created you to be just that, a wife. The question is – are you able to be married? God came to her and noticed her because she had marriage on her. What is drawing men's attention to you? Is it the look of marriage, or is it because of something else?

    Don't you know that you can go from uncovered to covered in an instant? Even when God sees our nakedness, He doesn't look at us in shame but He looks at us with mercy. No matter what you have done uncovered, He can easily wash all that dirt and shame away and cover you. The best part is that we are not entitled to have such notice from such a King, but to be cherished by Him is such an honor. To be regarded with love is so much more satisfying than to be seen with lust.

When the Lord comes into covenant with us there is no bond that is stronger. He said and you became Mine. Wow, to belong to Jesus, to be considered His own; now that is a privilege. Come to Him naked and unclothed and He will cover your nakedness up. He will restore you fully and you will become unabated.

When you love someone, you want them to be covered. You do not want them shamed or ashamed, so you cover their nakedness. This is shown in Genesis 9:20-23. Here Noah has become drunk from his vineyard and became uncovered in his tent. Two out of three sons cover him up and do not look upon him in that weak state. The same cannot be said of the other son.

Ham saw his father's nakedness and instead of laying a garment over him, he talked about it to others. Verse 22 says *"Ham, the father of Canaan, saw his father naked, and told his two brothers outside"* (Genesis 9:22, NIV). When it was told to them they quickly and quietly went in backwards, so not to see him, and placed a cover over him. That was exactly how the situation should have been handled. You never leave someone you love uncovered.

If a man looks at you for your body and not for what you embody, then he is not worthy of your time. This is only if you are actually representing who you truly are. You can sometimes get so comfortable in the counterfeit you, that you think you will spend the same. Sadly, this is not the case. If someone were to look closely at you, they would see the truth in the false perception you are trying to portray.

Romans clearly states *"Let not then your good be evil spoken of:"* (Romans 14:16). Do not allow what is a good thing inside of you be poisoned by others because you used it in a negative way. For example, I am a giver but I shouldn't have given myself away to anyone and everyone. I should have given myself only to my husband when marriage came. When you give away yourself in that manner no one says "oh, she is such a giver, just selfless." No, they talk about you in a bad way and call you fast and many other derogatory names.

The Bible says *"Abstain from all appearance of evil"* (1 Thessalonians 5:22). You have to stay away from anything that doesn't even seem right with God. Know that if it looks like sin, it can eventually lead to sin. Take a fire; it radiates heat, but if you get just close enough you will get burned. That is the same with sin; if you are tempted by it, it will not be long before you are actively participating in it.

Let's take a look at Adam and Eve. Eve was tempted by the serpent to eat of the tree of good and evil. She knew it was wrong because she almost quoted God verbatim, but she wanted it to be right. With one "it's ok," she no longer hesitated to do what she more than likely wanted to do the entire time. You cannot walk with somebody unless you agree and Adam, who was in agreement because he was there, ate right alongside her.

Notice this though; sin has a way of opening your eyes all right. In Genesis it says *"And they were both naked, the man and his wife, and were not ashamed"* (Genesis 2:25). Look at what happened after they ate the fruit. *"Then the eyes of both of them were opened, and they realized that they were naked; so they sewed fig leaves together and made coverings for themselves"* (Genesis 3:7, NIV). Where they were once innocent and blameless they became guilty and ashamed.

When their nakedness became evident they became humiliated by the sin and instead of repenting, they tried to cover it up. How many times do you do that? You sin and try to cover it up as if God doesn't already know what you have done? The thing you wanted so badly becomes the very thing that makes you fall. God knows all and He sees all. Once tainted by the color of sin, it is hard to erase what has been vibrantly colored in. Only God can uncover the sin and clean us up to cover us once again.

When they heard God walking in the garden they hid themselves from Him. Yes, when you are in Christ and you sin you may do this same thing, you try to hide. God is omniscient, so He is all knowing, He already knew what you were going to do before you even thought to do it. After it was all said and done they became afraid from the knowledge they received. Which brings me to this simple conclusion; what good is it to gain more knowledge if you won't use what you already know with obedience?

What you must do is to allow God to be your covering. Allow God access into those private areas and He will tend to you properly. Take down your "do not trespass sign" and He will lovingly birth life inside of you. Holy Spirit is a perfect gentleman in this sense, and He will show you how you are supposed to be loved. Once you have learned this area you can properly ascertain situations involving love.

Through His love you will come into the full knowledge of your worth. You will better comprehend that you are more than just a "dime piece." You will have the capacity to add up that your value cannot be equated to dollars or cents. God will give you the revelation that you are treasure that is buried in Him and the only person that will be handed that map is a man who will value you as such. Your worth is generated by God not man, and in understanding this you will get a man who will add to you, not one who subtracts from you.

You do not have to be validated by anyone but Christ and His thoughts are all that matter. I know the feeling of not being good enough for anyone to love, but that is a lie devised by the enemy to never allow you to amount to anything. Oh, but count it all joy, because what the devil meant for your bad God will make for your good. All of the times you felt at odds with yourself, God will subtract the negative and it will equal out to being better than you even totaled it out to be. Trust God, He is better at math than any of us. What takes time for you to figure out is simple mathematics to Him.

Are you willing to take responsibility for your actions? Do not be like Adam and Eve and have a typical response to sin. You cannot afford to shrug it off and pretend it doesn't exist. Stand bold and be brave and face the situation at hand. Not another day will go by of you hiding from the presence of the Lord.

Do not allow your sin to forever brand you as cursed. God is redeeming and can forgive you and give you new clothes. The rotten fruit can be replaced and good fruit can be produced. Do not uncover the truth of being in Him to only cover you up with the very thing that was deceiving. When Jesus saw the fig tree from afar it gave the perception that it had ripe fruit, but when He got close enough He saw it had nothing to offer him, so He cursed it. Adam and Eve covered themselves with those very leaves. Don't cover yourself in what is cursed but be untangled by the yoke of bondage and be made free.

Beauty Tips

In this section of beauty tips we will talk about lips. Everyday all day you are constantly using your mouth to speak and eat. These things are reoccurring, so it is vitally imperative that you take care of your mouth. Take care of your teeth as well because the best part of the smile is the pearly whites. Here are some tips for keeping your lips nice and healthy.

~Be sure to exfoliate your lips 1x a week, so that they stay smooth and supple.

~When wearing a matte lipstick be sure to condition your lips with a heavily moisturizer lip balm like Carmex. Blot off any excess before applying your matte lipstick.

~To help your lipstick last all day. First, apply a lip liner, then brush on setting powder with a fluffy brush, last, apply your lipstick. The extra layers act as a foundation for your lipstick to last.

A Simple Prayer

Here is a prayer to rebuke disease and learn to resist the enemy in lust.

Father God, thank you for who you are. Thank you for being my covering and keeping me protected. I ask for the gift of discernment to increase inside of me and began to help me in my area of struggle. Help me to know who is for me and who is not. In Jesus name I speak myself worth into existence. I decree that not another day will go by that I short change myself, but that I begin to add up my worth and know that it is more than just saved change. I thank you for your mercy toward me. I cultivate an atmosphere of praise and worship for you God, and I ask you to go where I go. Lead me down the paths of righteousness and keep me pure in your sight. I ask that you help me to change my outward appearance to be more in line with who you are inside of me. Let me match your light, Lord God, and keep me walking uprightly before you, God. Let me find my worth in you, Jesus, and keep me covered by your wing. Thank you for claiming me and giving me wisdom to stay away from the things not like you. I even praise you for changing my ways, oh Lord. I thank you that my body belongs only to you and that I am no longer giving myself away to others. Give me the strength to resist the devil that he might flee. I will stay in your presence Jesus and I will give this battle over to you. For I know that this battle does not belong to me, and I know that by your stripes I am already healed. I decree and declare that no matter or form of disease can reside inside of me. My body is your temple and my life I give as a living sacrifice. Clean me up for your using, God, have your way inside of me.

In Jesus name, Amen.

Chapter 10

The Problem with Rejection

Have you ever felt rejected? I am sure at some point we all have gone through some form or another of rejection. Rejection is a very hard thing to deal with, and in my opinion is the easiest way to lead to low self-esteem. This is the way the enemy creeps in and manipulates us to believe his lie. Today we will break that spirit of rejection off of your life.

We all will face a time where we will find ourselves in the weird predicament where something can make us or break us. It is up to you to decide if it is going to break you or hopefully make you. I have noticed that people who deal strongly with offense find themselves suffering from rejection the most. Let me help you with something; every person is not going to like you. Every person is not going to agree with your ideas and views on things, but who cares?

God has given us all an audience. He has given everyone a reach of some sort. Your arms may be longer than mine but I will be content in whom my arms can encircle. You have to understand that *"To the weak became I as weak, that I might gain the weak: I am made all things to all men, that I might by all means save some"* (1 Corinthians 9:22). If you have to be ridiculed and rejected to win some, then so be it. By any means necessary you must fulfill your charge.

You have to love regardless. I wrote recently on Facebook, "Love with all of your being because there is healing in love." When loving the end result may be rejection but one thing that I know for sure is this: *"Above all things have fervent charity among yourselves: for charity shall cover the multitude of sins"* (1 Peter 4:8). When you love deeply that love can and will cover sins. Love is a healing agent and it will release you from the grip of rejection.

What is rejection? Rejection is the act of not accepting, believing, or considering something. For you to confront rejection you have to get out of the need for approval and applause. When you begin to care less what others think, you will begin to care more about what God thinks. Honestly, that is all that matters.

You may not be a prophet to the nations, but like the Lord told Jeremiah, *"Before I formed thee in the belly, I knew thee; and before thou camest forth out of the womb I sanctified thee, and I ordained thee a prophet unto the nations" (Jeremiah 1:5)* Before you were born, He set you apart for His holy purpose. That scripture is for us all. He set you apart; He called you to be different. God has given you purpose; you just have to believe that you have a purpose to pursue.

The problem with rejection is that it causes you to eject yourself from the promises of God. Once rejection finds a doorway it sets up shop inside you and plans out all the missed opportunities it is waiting to make happen. Rejection is the biggest bubble popper and dream snatcher. It is the main destiny killer and the quickest thief to your hopes out there. It will rob you of happiness and self-confidence and just ruin your life.

Rejection is the aftertaste of negativity. It is painful and cutting. It pierces through your heart and can halt all great expectations. Being rejected is embarrassing at times and quite uncomfortable for the victim. If this is a constant in your life, you can move beyond it.

Be encouraged because Jesus was not received in His own home town and there He could perform no mighty works. Many that know you may become too familiar with you, and may easily reject you, but don't let it affect your witness. Keep praying for them because God said that any voice that rises up against you he will condemn. Your witness is the greatest tool you have and if you allow rejection to stop you from using it, you have just done yourself and others a great disservice. Since rejection is a tool, keep on using it to build.

Rejection is not a death walk because God will never allow us to walk alone. Remember, *"Yea though I walk through the valley of the shadow of death, I will fear no evil: for thou art with me; thy rod and thy staff they comfort me"* (Psalm 23:4). Yes, in the midst of it all, God is with you. He knows rejection far better than we ever could, and because of that you can go to Him and His embrace will always be welcoming. He has covered your shame and rejection with His precious blood.

Having rejection can cause you to want to build walls up around your heart, so no one can ever get inside again. Rejection loves to construct those walls, but those walls are to keep you locked in and introduce isolation to you. Those walls will only bring you to a lonely place and shut out all the possibilities of life. Rejection can be quite cancerous because it is filled with negativity and self-pity. Bulldoze those walls and demolish the onset of rejection by freeing yourself from the cares of the world. *"What shall we then say tothese things? If God be for us, who can be against us"* (Romans 8:31).

Rejection is, to me, the worst trigger to low self-esteem because it delivers a direct blow to your confidence. It can give you a brutal beating. If you do not know how to defend yourself and throw counter punches, rejection just might get the win. When dealing with rejection you have to throw jabs. You must become fully extended.

Stretch forth in prayer; let your reach be fully extended. Do not stop reaching for the true things, and duck from the hand of the enemy. Each morning you must put on the full armor of God and go forth being prepared for anything. Start each day in prayer, never ceasing throughout the day as well. Keep His word etched in your heart and you will withstand the fiery darts of Satan.

Rejection takes away your sense of belonging. Yes, you do need people. I know it has been said that it is better to do badly by yourself, but maybe if you had someone around with a positive personality it would counter react your negativity and cause a better mood to develop inside of you. Of course you want to be loved and feel accepted. That is a desire inside of us all.

Inside of the presence of God you are accepted. Once you come into covenant with Him you become an heir with Christ. He calls you His own, His beloved and in Him you do have a place to belong. His love will never fail; it goes on forever. He is and was and always will be, so never wonder or fret, He has enough love to last beyond this lifetime.

Rejection, sadly, is a part of life; of course when you are going through being rejected it feels anything but normal. The truth is that the probability of being rejected is usually far higher than the probability of being accepted. When applying to Harvard how many really believe they are going to be accepted? That is because more get rejection letters than get acceptance letters. Does it kill these individuals? No. Sure, it hurts, but they move on to the next school they like.

When interviewing for a new job, do you always get the position? Have you ever been told they found someone who was more qualified? How about they just didn't even call to tell you yes or no about the job? That is all very much rejection but we move on and look for a new job. We may have wanted that exact job but we understand that we don't always get the job or make it into the school we want. That doesn't mean that "no" defines quit.

Never give up, don't throw in the towel. Rejection is just redirection. It helps you to get a fresh look at everything and inspires you to find another choice and it just might be the better choice. Rejection is like the sign on the road that says "detour." Yes, let it lead you down a different route but to the same destination. Who said you had to follow life's map? As long as you allow God to be the traffic director you will be fine.

How can you protect yourself from rejection? Rejection can actually be used as protection. Yes, it can literally help you in seeing the truth for what it is. Sometimes we have to admit that we were wrong and maybe it just wasn't good. It is that simple; maybe your best wasn't good enough.

That doesn't mean you aren't good or great. Just because you didn't win the Science fair doesn't mean that your project was rejected because it was horrible. Maybe someone was more creative, followed instructions better or didn't wait until the last possible moment to do it. They could have presented it more clearly or precisely than you. That doesn't mean you invite rejection in, because it is not your friend, it is a loser looking for a hand out. There will always be someone whose skills are above yours, but there are also those whose skills are less than yours. You must learn from the first, and teach from the second.

Allow rejection to give you a reason for inspection. Yes, look at yourself in the mirror and use that negativity to find the great in you. You do not have to stay defeated. You can take all that negativity and use it as energy to improve. Better yourself for tomorrow.

The End to My Story...

I just kept myself busy. I was reading my word and trying to pray. I was taking care of my daughter and just working to provide for her. I had promised myself to God and was serious about living devoted to Him. My prayer to God was that He would help me get even closer to Him.

I had no clue at that time what he was going to do to make that happen, but I left it in His hands. God is a good God and He is no respector of persons, so when He does something He does it right. The funniest part is the Lord has an entirely different plan then we usually do. I love when He disrupts my regular scheduled programming with His public service announcements. God definitely gave me the surprise of my life.

It was a cold February day and I was just getting into the groove at work. At this time, I was working at a vision center as an optician. I happened to look up from my computer and across the room I met eyes with a silhouette of God's beauty. Yes, there was this man that just radiated with light, sitting at a desk across the room, staring at me. I was uncomfortable because there was this light about him, but I was drawn to him nevertheless.

I went about my business and when I next looked up he was gone. He came back a couple of days later, and when I saw him I smiled and waved. I remembered him quite easily. I mean who could forget someone who radiated light the way he did. He was assisted by another person on my team, but I felt his presence the entire time he was out there. He went in to see the doctor and when he came back out, she gave his chart to me.

He wanted to try contacts, and had never worn them before. I was there to teach him how to properly wear contacts and to take care of them. He was by far the hardest person I ever taught in that area. He just couldn't do it for anything. Every time the contact on his finger came even an inch in front of his eye he would quickly close it. I mean this man's reflexes were amazing.

The entire time I was instructing him, he was talking to me. He was pouring out of his spirit his love for God and the things of God. I was intrigued to say the least but it was more because of his pure admiration to Christ. It was something I had never seen from a man; I mean he wore his heart on his sleeve for Jesus. It was very refreshing to witness that public display of affection for God.

FINDING ME IN THE MESS

After all the teaching and explaining was over, he still wasn't able to get the contacts in or out, so he was going to come back and look for glasses. I gave him my number and kindly asked him to please help me with my walk with God and send me scriptures and stuff on God. He left and then came back with a flyer for his church. I thought about our conversation all day and was even more excited to run after God. I never knew then that my life would forever change from that initial experience with that man.

He called me that very night. I was so surprised because that goes against everything I had ever known a guy to do. Men never call the first day; it breaks all the rules. He was a man like no other and he was the exception to every rule ever created. This man was different and it showed.

We talked into the wee hours of the morning. We talked and conversed all about Jesus. He told me how he came into the body of Christ and asked all about my dreams and ambitions. It was easy to talk to him and share with him. I was more than comfortable with this man, we just fit together. He was the missing piece to my unfinished puzzle.

Time went on and wounds began to heal. We got closer and closer because I began to walk closer to God. Things that seemed out of place were starting to realign and hopes began to resurface. My once icy heart was starting to thaw and a new season was quickly approaching. My cold winter month of a frozen heart, a hard ground and a cold demeanor were fading fast, and new was starting to come forth.

I was blossoming into who God created me to be and it felt good. This man had changed my life by introducing God to me in a way I had never known Him. Our relationship was so Christ centered that we didn't know where he and I began to where God started. The Lord was that infused into our love story; we truly had a three strand chord. I was really in a good place.

It didn't take long for us to know we wanted forever with one another. He asked me to marry him only four months after our first date and six months later we were married. That was over 7 years ago that I met the man that would forever change my life. I never knew God would answer my prayer to go deeper in Him by bringing me my husband. What God has for you is truly for you, and that was the good plan he had for me.

I am thankful that I was obedient and never sacrificed on the commitment and pledge I made to Jesus that day. I truly longed to know Him and by my invitation to know Him greater He sent a RSVP and arrived to my party of one. He gave me the best present one could ever receive…life! He gave me abundant life; He gave me a hope and a future. God showed up in my life and showed sin the exit sign.

Today I stand before you renewed, revived and completely whole. I am a woman of God, a wife and a mother. There is nothing that is too hard for God. When you hand God the broken pieces of you, only He can fix what He created with precision. He truly is a miracle worker.

God not only corrected what was unaligned, but He put air in my tires. He vacuumed and cleaned up my inside and gave me the fragrance of Him. Jesus washed my outside and made me presentable to become a daughter of The King. He placed a crown of victory upon my head. My God, my savior, The King of kings…He gave me my royalty and I know that I am precious in His sight.

My story ends here on paper but it will continue on in the strength of the Lord our God. My story was made for His glory and He gets all the praise. Low self-esteem has to flee because it is not of God and it has no place in what belongs to Him. I pray that this small part of my testimony helps you to believe you are more than a conqueror and that the plans of satan can have no affect over your life, if you allow God to take control. If you give your heart over to Jesus, know this; He will never ever break it. May you be restored and forever made whole in our Lord and savior Jesus Christ.

(Healing)

Showing Rejection Your Reflection

"Therefore if any man is in Christ, he is a new creature: old things are passed away; behold, all things are become new" (**2 Corinthians 5:17**).

This is by far one of my most favorite scriptures, for these words ring so crisp and true. This is a forever change. Your old life is gone and new life has just begun. The brand new has shown up on the scene; you have come into being. The NEW has surely come!

This scripture means you have been renewed. You are now a redeemed woman. This means much more than an outward reformation but an inward manifestation of God's workmanship should be crafted in you. You have been reconciled unto Christ. You have finally stopped knowing Him through your flesh but by way of the spirit. You have been introduced to YOU, the real you.

You have to put on your new self. In the Bible it says *"And to put on the new self, created to be like God in true righteousness and holiness"* (Ephesians 4:24, NIV). Therefore, be a new creation. You may look like you are the same person but your character and conduct will be different. We were His desired design but we fell and now we are able to be made the righteousness of God.

Would you go out in a blizzard without a coat? No, you would put on a coat to be prepared for the conditions of the weather. When you put ON (key word there is on) your new self, you are putting Christ on. You are now ready to withstand the conditions of the weather. You can now go out and battle the elements more efficiently because you are wearing the correct gear.

With new we must walk out of old. We have to walk right past the past. The scripture above says old things are passed away. This means that they are dead and gone. Old goes, so that new can come.

With each new spring the snow melts and is gone. Once it has left there is no evidence that it was ever there. Yes, sometimes the snow lingers and it takes awhile for the new to be seen. The good news is that a new season has come in and new life will begin to spring forth out of your inner man. Your cold and lonely season is over, and blossoms and sweet aromas are being born out of your spirit. Look expectantly into your future.

Learn from the word of God *"Forget the former things; do not dwell on the past "*(Isaiah 43:18, NIV). Forget what used to be. Never mind what once was. That is no longer a concern. You are brand new and rightly so.

Do not allow your mind to replay the past to you. When we are forgiven and have accepted Jesus as our Lord and Savior, He has already washed all of our sins away. They are no more and He remembers them not. You must, as well, cast them from your memory. Do not allow road blocks to keep you from your appointed destination.

Reflect on where you once were, but reflect only to go forward. Never get in a mindset of "I will go back to Egypt" because it isn't exactly going as you planned. The children of Israel did the same thing and because of their complaining they never made it to the place called there. Do not allow a short journey to turn into forty years stagnation. Do not miss your promise because of rejection.

It is time that you finally stand up and take a deep breath. Walk with your head high and look yourself dead in the mirror. It is time you show rejection your reflection. It is time you look it right in its eye and show it you mean business. You no longer have to be defeated, for you are triumphant.

You have overcome, yes, you are an overcomer. You have overcome the snares of the enemy. When he tried to trap you, you found a way out of it. When he attempted to assassinate your character, you took a moment to pray and kept it moving. When he thought he would plague your mind with negative, you focused in on God and brought every thought into the captivity of Christ.

Yes, you are a conqueror. When the mountain was standing tall you had faith and cast it down into the sea. As you sat in the lion's den you stood on God's word and every mouth of your enemies was closed. Yes, the Lord condemned every tongue and not one mouth could open. When the fires of the world's furnace turned up on you, you stood firmly planted and God showed up and showed out with you as everyone watched in shock that you were still alive.

You, beautiful woman of God, are triumphant. Yes, you are, because you stepped out of that boat and dared to walk on water despite the storm around you. You stood sure in you and despite what others saw or thought you went and faced the giant called low self-esteem. Yes, it was huge and it looked undefeatable. Yet you faced it and knew the only thing you needed was a stone. That one and only rock called Jesus, and you used your arsenal like only you knew how. You trusted on your Lord and He delivered you out of the hands of your enemy.

What a mighty woman, a defender for all women everywhere. Run like the woman at the well and tell of this man who told you everything about yourself. The Bible says we are overcome by the blood of the lamb and the word of our testimony. You must now go out and share how you overcame low self-esteem. Share so that others can be inspired and understand that without God there is no way out.

Oh, but when we are in Jesus there is a light at the end of the tunnel. He shines in our darkness and shows us the way out. He guides us when we are lost, so that we may once again be found. He will never leave nor forsake us but will always be by our side. A constant help in trouble and He always sticks closer than a brother.

Now, that you are able to look at yourself in the mirror, what do you see? Do you see that you are beautiful because He hand crafted you? Queen, do you see your worth? God created you as royalty. Nothing can compare to you for you are most precious to God.

It reads in Proverbs *"She is more precious than rubies: and all the things thou canst desire are not to be compared unto her"* (Proverbs 3:15) It said compare nothing to her, **NOTHING**. No precious and sought after gem can ever match your splendor. You are the belle of the ball, the apple of His eye. You are worth more than any fancy jewel could ever amount to.

Look at yourself and look deeply. Close your eyes and see you. Not the vanity appearance of you, but the real you, the one God says you are. Take a moment and acquaint yourself with you. There are many different artificial sweeteners but real sugar comes from sugar cane. It cannot be duplicated and neither can you. You are needed in your natural form because others can tell the difference.

Give yourself a pat on the back because low self-esteem just got served. Yes, you just told it to pack up because you will no longer stay with anything that is low. Your standards are too high and it doesn't qualify. Low level thinking doesn't meet your standards. Hold your head high and smile.

Now, you can walk in confidence. Now, you can smile. You are proof that the enemy can never win. You are a living testament to God's glorious power. A woman with a purpose may you always be a reflection of God's perfection.

Did you know that reflections are powerful things? Do you know that your reflection carries enough of God's light to light up others around you? The sun sets as the moon rises. As the moon rises you still see outside quite well because it has light illuminating out of it. That light though is the light of the sun reflecting off the moon's surface.

God shines enough of His light in you to reflect outwardly. His light is bright enough to be seen from afar. Light attracts and darkness must flee. Your reflection should now be lighting up the path for others to get out of that darkness. Your surface should be reflecting the love of God who is inside you and radiating it out for others to bask in its warmth.

Look inside of yourself and pull you out. Take your God ordained authority and get yourself free. No more of being stuck by low self-esteem. Sing and dance and give praise unto God, for you have found what you were looking for. You can finally say these words, "I found me! Though the mess was much, I found ME!"

Beauty Tips

These set of tips are for fitness. When you are healthy, everything else is healthier. You look younger and more vibrant. Healthiness leads to a longer life and a much better quality of living. Here are some helpful tips for you to use.

~Make one change at a time… get used to that one thing before you add. Slow and steady wins the race.

~If you fall off the wagon, it's not the end of the road, you can get back up and keep going. Even the most conditioned athletes find themselves starting over again, it's okay!

~Do 1 thing EVERYDAY no matter how small to reach your goals. Some days will be busier than others, but nothing is too small or insignificant.

A Simple Prayer

This prayer will help you uproot and cancel every spirit that low self-esteem tried to send to you.

Father God I give you glory. Lord I lift you up on high. I thank you that I have overcome. I thank you that I am victorious over this strong hold in my life. Low self-esteem, I curse you at the root. You are void and of no effect in Jesus name. I uproot you and I cut down every spirit connected to you.

I uproot and cancel objectification

I uproot and cancel guilt

I uproot and cancel depression

I uproot and cancel isolation

I uproot and cancel pride

I uproot and cancel shyness

I uproot and cancel promiscuity

I uproot and cancel rejection

I take authority given to me by my Father in heaven and I cut these things at the root. I speak life over me. I decree and declare that wholeness be my portion. Let it be so now in the name of Jesus. Lord, I ask for continued release from this spirit. I am made new today and I thank you that I am free. I thank you that I am a new creation. You found me in the mess and gave me a clean slate. Thank you Lord.

In Jesus name, Amen.

Epilogue

In conclusion, this book is to help you find your self-confidence and to keep it. In the word mess you see the word ME. Despite the mess around you, there is a ME in it all. Clean up the mess and find you in it all. Understand that you are going to make mistakes but just don't get comfortable sitting in that mess but rather get up, pick yourself up, dust yourself off and keep on moving.

Your beauty isn't validated by the mess that is right now. Roses are some of the most beautiful flowers in the entire world but growing them is quite a hassle and can become a difficult task. You need patience, time, dedication and band aids. Roses can be unruly and time consuming because you have to constantly be out there cutting weeds and keeping insects at bay and trying to maintain the wildness of the roses. You also have to keep band aids handy because of the cuts you can get trying to tame them.

Roses are so exquisite; they are classic and timeless. They represent love and beauty among other things. Roses are full of wonder and awe but yet they have thorns. Though those thorns prick a person, that has never stopped people from wanting to hold them and capture the sweet fragrance of its petals. What I am saying is even though you feel your mess will turn people away from you; you will soon see that you will be loved regardless of the mess.

Your beauty is as breath taking as the roses is. You may not see what you are blossoming into, but when you bloom you will see the mess was just a process. The mess was a place for you to become everything you are today. We all have to go through the fiery furnace to come out pure gold. No, it doesn't feel good but it is necessary. Though you may bloom gradually, eventually you will unfold all of your glorious layers. You are intricate as you are elegant, find the beauty in that.

    Don't let your moment of mess define you for the rest of your life. Look deep inside and know that you are better than that junk and believe in yourself and bloom anyway. Bloom into who God created you to be. Look through all of what's around you and find who God says that you are. Treasure what you find and know that you found you inside of God and be free in that knowledge. When it's all said and done, you will no longer have low self-esteem. You will finally be able to proudly say, "Through the process, despite the mess, I found ME".

> **"Confidence is birthed out of breaking out of the confines of the mind"**
>
> **EKS**

POETRY

By: Emily ~K~ Strickland

"DIAMONDS"

I was locked up and looked over, completely covered in my dirt. I was locked up in my own mind by confusion which led to hurt. Looked over because I was lying in my mess, devaluing my worth, but yet to my unknowing, God was doing a work.

Lost in a world of my being an introvert, for I thought if I didn't speak there was no way for temptation to be perked... inside me... ...so I allowed me to become... lifeless!! Put forget-me-nots inside my heart but never giving my heart, so I forgot that not I, but His will be done, for His life is priceless!

I was completely off balance, so unstable back then because I was spineless... I as well had no common sense for I was mindless. And I was incapable of spreading my wings, which left me flightless and my vision was lacking because I was so sightless. I was constantly uneasy with worry, which made me restless, but then God hit me in my lungs and took out all my air and left me breathless, and then my heart began to beat to the beat of His drum and He told me "you can get through this," and walking through affliction taught me to be...selfless!!

So less of self, I put me on the shelf and focused on Him, digging deeper and deeper until I was lost in His abyss! Fighting what was my sin of silence with the volumes of His holiness! Blowing up what was in me lying dormant with the power of His explosiveness and gained my smile and intelligence back because I knew I was in His knowingness!

And the chains began to break… the structure of sins foundation in me began to shake… and like Paul, God opened up the prisons gates of captivity within me and snatched me from that place… He set me free because I wanted to be! See, when you have no holding back, God will place you in front of the enemy within yourself, and he will scream, "ATTACK," and you have to battle and war until you truly know without a doubt that you have no lack and that you will never go back! You will win for it says in Corinthians 15:57 *"But thanks be to God, which giveth us the victory through our Lord Jesus Christ"*. And since you can do all things through Christ who strengthens you, you can get your life right too.

And He will take you from mess to simply the best! He will dig you up from the mud and wipe off the dirt and will show you to the world. For once you were just a pebble, a stone, but He gave you a new name and placed you at the foot of His throne. And when revealed you will see that though once all you saw was nothing, that when you stay focused on overcoming, you will look at yourself and only see who you're becoming. You… you're stunning and easily you will say, "I am beautiful, strong and vibrant". Because He washed away the rubble and He took you from hiding and showed you that the reason why you rock is because you're really a diamond!

"BREATHLESS"

I was slowly dying… losing myself; my heart was faintly beating. I was unconscious in movement… walking steadily in forward retreating. Not to any knowledge of my own thinking… treading water to only realize I was sinking. At war with myself and my battleship was sunk… shipwrecked left me recklessly about to take that plunge, so I jumped… overboard into the icy cold water. Hoping that the shock would somehow alter… this state of unbelief and God would send relief and somehow rescue me, but to my unawareness, I was in too deep…

Trying to save others and how quickly I lost me. Seeds of negativity skillfully planted within. Not realizing that saying nothing allowed me to become accustomed to that sin. Trying to be a friend, I'd pull out their weeds, leaving my garden untamed. Judging me not, I got lost in flowers and weeds looking the same.

Never pulling out the plank from my own eye first but how easily I saw their speck…like I didn't need any help, never realizing that what I was seeing was the reflection of the effect of sin inside myself. This is why I lost my insurance when my vehicle got wrecked. Put on trial for vehicular manslaughter and I the number one suspect. For it was time I slaughtered me in the things that I accept and killed myself until only God through me I could project.

So, I poured out me until there was nothing left. For there was nothing I wanted more than for Him to put me under arrest. In being empty I asked Him to fill me up. As His structure only He could reconstruct. So, He the potter and I the clay… all I could say was "Lord, have your way". I felt Him spinning me… molding me…

cutting me... holding me...He never let me go, as I went through process He was truly making me gold.

As I cried out I give you all of me... just take everything, all I am, all my dreams and all my plans. I place my life firmly in your hands. I was so embarrassed to be in His presence, for I felt so unworthy. For all the times He had to give me mercy. For all the times I forgot to pray, for all the times I too quickly complained. For living one way outside and another way inside the church, for all the people I unintentionally hurt.

Why would He still love me? How could He still want me? I stood there confessing my heart to His heart and the coldness of frost inside me began to melt. Somehow I was dying to my flesh, and His love I truly felt. No more toxic waste... No more saving face... no more running a rat race. But this time I shined from grace.

Before, I was fruitless because of the smallest fox. This time I took God out of the box. Now my branches are budding and my flowers will bloom. I am freshly scented by the fragrance of His holy perfume. I will walk God, talk God and my countenance will always bear His name. Before you speak negativity into me, God reflecting in me will convict you to feel ashamed.

So, once I was dying; my heart no longer about to beat. There was no pep in my step... no run in my feet. But He snatched me up in a chariot of fire... and said "you will not die here, it is time to go higher". And in that moment there was a gush of wind I didn't see it, but it was His breath of life blowing new life inside of me. And I felt myself falling into what is endless... now; I truly understand His love is so precious. For I will never be the same and forever I will remain; inside His heart beating one with my heart... leaving me...breathing... breathless.

FINDING ME IN THE MESS

"ADOOR"

So, I closed my door, for I was a house abandoned.

They kicked me in, broke me down and left my heart ransomed.

I was reduced to just an entrance, so they entered at will.

I was wide open, nothing to keep out that cold chill.

So I added an exit sign that flashed… "Exit only".

Eventually, that just left me lonely.

I thought it would be better to have them not enter at all; rather than have my heart broken into pieces with loves suicidal fall.

So miserable with them loving me and dumping me.

Yet, found out that the pain doesn't take away from the fact that misery loves company.

So I put up an emergency door, thinking they would stay, unless they had a desperate situation.

But they still came just to leave and I came to the realization the only desperate thing was me.

So I took down the door and put up some curtains made of lace.

But that was too risqué and caused them to treat me in a worse type of way.

And they just pimped my place, bringing other girls into my space.

FINDING ME IN THE MESS

And they'd just knock me down… pull me down… rip me down with no apology.

Just carelessly to pick me up and hang me haphazardly.

So I put in a screen door, with regal and rust.

But somehow my house still got filled with dust.

They cared very little and my screen became torn.

By this time, I was weary and worn.

So I put in something I thought would weather the storm.

But the storm door didn't keep out the rain, it seemed the better I tried to do, the more inside me it poured.

I was losing my wealth, and me I couldn't afford.

So I put in a patio door that slid back and forth.

But that put me on a sliding scale and counterfeited my worth.

I was now their relaxing place, someone with whom they chill.

 I was just a friend; not someone they truly feel.

I made it easy for them to have one foot out and one foot in.

I wanted real love, not just a friend.

So I put in a French door, just to give myself some class.

The sunlight poured through the length of my glass.

Its rays shined through my exterior, lighting up my interior.

FINDING ME IN THE MESS

The beauty of my outward door left me on the inside feeling inferior.

So I removed the door, decided I wanted no more, because I was bruised so deep within my core.

Lost myself in a dream world and my house became a castle, and me a draw bridge, and I was only going to let it down when my prince came.

But that just let me down because how quickly I found they were all the same.

So waiting for my prince… left me a damsel in distress.

Lost in what I couldn't handle, left me a complete mess.

So I woke up and stepped back into reality.

Realized I had subtracted myself so much that I couldn't add up in totality.

Then I understood I had to sit still and wait on God's will.

Though once empty, with God His love in me filled.

So now just a frame but blessed beyond belief along he came.

A man with structure and a plan, and he built me from the ground up with his very own hands.

He knocked down the walls and opened me up.

That allowed me to see inside myself, so I could know his love.

FINDING ME IN THE MESS

He took the wood that had splintered my heart, sanded it down to give me a fresh start.

He took the window that bluntly showcased the world and colored it in with mother of pearl.

He fashioned me a lock of bronzy brass, and only if you held the key could you enter and pass.

He also built in a peep hole, so I could see who knocked.

If I didn't want to let them in, I could just keep my door locked.

He as well installed a doorbell and his melody rang in my soul.

My builder, my love, who was instructed to construct me bold.

He painted the post around my door in bright red.

Now, colored by Gods covering, all the enemies fled.

I went from rejected to respected, from projecting pain to protecting my name.

And my property value began to soar…all because God saw the possibility in my door.

He said not just a door but adore… for we have to adore who we are, and find what our purpose is for.

Now, I believe you can make a house a home.

Not by putting on bravado in public and then crying alone.

Not by proving you are super woman, and doing it all on your own.

FINDING ME IN THE MESS

But by putting on the whole armor of God and using the knowledge you were given.

Like being anxious for nothing like Sarah and filling your heart with joy and out of your mouth will flow laughter.

Then you will find yourself amused while you're waiting on your happily ever after.

Or there's a verse that says come boldly before the throne, so learn to be brave as Esther charting into areas unknown.

Yet, remember she always represented herself tastefully and gracefully, and that is why she was able to come unsummoned before the king's throne.

You're beautiful, confident, incredible and intelligent; you do not have to compromise.

God knows the desires of your heart and will bring someone who exactly fits your size.

Remember as a woman, you are the opening, the entryway…the door.

Keep your entrance clear and your house holy, adore yourself and keep your door adorned… with love, kindness and understanding than you will never have to be a woman scorned, but only a woman of virtue, honor and difference… a door outside the norm.

A Call To Repentance

Did you know that seeing yourself as less than what God called you to be is a sin? As long as we are content to live in sin, the Bible says that we are separated from God. Sometimes in life we don't notice that we are separated from Him, but as time goes by we eventually feel this void in our life, and we try to fill it with everything... love, cars, houses, etc., but it will remain a hole until we fill it with Christ. He is the only one who can fix that hole, by making us whole. If you would be willing right now to admit that you need a new start, the God of second chances desires to give you just that. All you have to do is repeat these words...

"Father, I know that I have broken your laws and my sins have separated me from you. I am truly sorry, and now I want to turn away from my past sinful ways toward you. Lord, please, forgive me, and help me to be guided away from sin. I believe that your son, Jesus Christ died for me, was resurrected from the dead, and is alive today. I invite Jesus to become The Lord of my life, to rule in my heart from this day forward. I ask that you send your Holy Spirit to help me obey you, and to always do your will for the rest of my life. In Jesus name, Amen."

If you just prayed that prayer with me, you have been made brand new. You must steward this new life, and guard your heart with all diligence. I would advise you to find a church where you can be with like-minded believers that will help you grow in Christ. Talk to them about being baptized, it is necessary and God ask that we do this. Remember to pray and study your word, this will sharpen you in Him. I love you with the love of The Lord and once again, welcome to Christ family.

Acknowledgements

I would like to first acknowledge my Lord and savior, Jesus Christ for giving me the words to write this book. I thank you God, for being there for me every step of my life, you truly deserve all the glory. I pray this book lifts you up so high, and draws lost souls home to you.

I want to honor my husband Chaz, you my love, are so deserving of praise. You sat and let me rattle off thoughts for this book, dealt with me when I would get upset at it not coming out right. You pushed me when I wanted to quit and truly believed in me the entire time. For everything you do, I thank you, and I love you.

To my 4 babies, I love you guys so much. My world would seem empty without God giving me each one of you. Thank you for putting up with me.

Thanks to my family, my mom Leslie, for always being there to listen and helping me stay focused. Thanks to my sisters and brother Stef, Melinda, Bryan and Kari, I love you guys.

To my mother in love Jamariea, I love you, thank you for all your encouragement.

To my friends Aja and Veronica, you two were a great support system while writing this book, and always through anything I do, thank you both so much. Veronica, you did amazing on my cover. Thank you.

Special thanks to my friend Peggy Ruh who is the Studio Manager over at Life Time Fitness at the Pickerington, Ohio location. Thank you for your contribution on the fitness tips, I love you lady.

As well, a special thanks to my friend Brittany Bradley, who is a Licensed Cosmetologist, specializing in hair and makeup. You can email her at Brittanykbradley@aol.com. Thank you for your beauty tips on hair and makeup, love you honey!!

A huge thank you goes out to Charlie, for editing my book. You are awesome, and I adore you.

To my church family at Ignite, I love each one of you so much. Thank you guys for believing in me, and trusting me with a part of your spiritual walk, I do not take it lightly.

ABOUT THE AUTHOR

Emily Strickland is a dynamic and humble woman after God's own heart. She is a wife and mother, and she believes very strongly that her family is her first ministry. Emily began serving Jesus fully and totally at age 24. She was radically changed after finding Jesus Christ. Since that experience she carries a holy fire, and a need to bring revival to the world. Emily is a prophetess and operates under the power of The Holy Spirit. She ministers strongly in healing and deliverance. God has called her as a mouth piece to this generation. Emily is an example of God's power being able to transform anyone's life. She is a voice of healing to women that have gone through traumatic experiences. Her goal is to uplift and empower people through the word of God, and see their lives forever changed. She alongside her husband Chazdon Strickland are the founders of Ignite Church Revival Center. They have 4 children and are currently residing in Florida.

If you would like to reach out to her you can email her at redeemedvoicepublishing@yahoo.com

Made in the USA
Middletown, DE
22 March 2022